STRATEGIC MANAGEMENT IN EAST EUROPEAN PORTS

T0358529

To Andrea, Horst, Isabell, Usi, Dr Ozanosy,
Liz, Joe and Siân

Strategic Management in East European Ports

SUSANNE FERCH AND MICHAEL ROE
Institute of Marine Studies
University of Plymouth

Routledge
Taylor & Francis Group

LONDON AND NEW YORK

blishing

lon, Oxon, OX14 4RN
0017, USA

r & Francis Group, an informa business

998

trademarks or registered trademarks, and
explanation without intent to infringe.

gths to ensure the quality of this reprint
ections in the original copies may be

t to trace copyright holders and welcomes
ve been unable to contact.

under LC control number: 98072803

Contents

Lists of tables and figures

List of tables

List of figures

List of appendices

Summary

Following the transformation of Poland and later of the remainder of Eastern Europe, Polish ports faced not only economic instability and uncertainty in their business environment but also changing trade patterns, a free market economy, sudden and fierce competition and the beginnings of privatisation prescribed by the state. Together, these all contributed to making the business environment even more turbulent.

This research text investigates how the two largest ports of Poland, the Port of Gdynia and the Port of Gdańsk use strategic management techniques in the hope of gaining competitive advantage well into the 21st century.

The focus of the study is the process of strategy, i.e. its elements and strategic management systems. The aim is to determine whether and how, the highly turbulent environment is reflected in the ports' strategic management systems. Particular attention is paid to inter-port variations, if any, since both ports operate in the same business environment and are located almost in the same location.

The results showed that respondents primarily think in terms of content when they refer to strategy. The process of strategy crafting is not formalised and involves only few and generally senior managers.

This study supports the notion that if western standards were taken as a measure, many a field of port strategic management in Poland would be seen to lie fallow.

Acknowledgements

This text emerged from a research study conducted through the Institute of Marine Studies at the University of Plymouth, led by Susanne Ferch and with a contribution from myself. It represents a collaboration involving a number of close contacts from the Polish maritime sector to whom we both offer our thanks.

Susanne would like to express her gratitude to the staff of the Institute of Marine Studies for creating the academic atmosphere in which this research was undertaken - and especially to Harry Heijveld and Jeff Usher, sources of intellectual support and challenge. She is indebted to Huw Dobson, Peter Marlow and Stephen Pettit of MASTS at the University of Cardiff, who generously enabled her to undertake research in their library. Also thanks to all the Polish port officials as well as Professor Leopold Kuzma, Professor Stanislaw Szwankowski, Professor Andrzej Tubielwicz and Professor Wlodimirz Rydzkowski for their time and shared insights. Dr Dagmar Felix of the University of Passau, charismatic tutor and subsequent employer is also thanked for her constant encouragement during undergraduate studies and her constant help.

As everyone always says at the annual Oscar ceremonies and at this stage of any book, it would be impossible to thank everyone involved in its production but as usual one or two people stand out. My thanks go in particular to Aleks Wrona in Zabianka for her consistently entertaining emails and the concept of Gierek style interior design; and as always to Marie Bendell here in Plymouth for her uncomplaining work on some of the horrendously complicated appendices and her continuing commitment to everything I do.

A constant inspiration this year has been the form of the finest football team - Charlton Athletic - who currently lie in third place in the Nationwide League Division One, heading for at least a play-off place. It is particularly gratifying considering the tiny amount of money spent on new players compared with others in the division and in contrast to the traumas at the end of the late 1980s. One hopes that the richer teams predominantly in the Premiership, one day might understand that football is a lot more than satellite television, South American imports, replica shirts and supporters who have never actually seen the team.

Michael Roe, Plymouth
April 29th, 1998.

List of abbreviations

BCG Boston Consulting Group
BCT Baltic Container Terminal
BTDG Baltic General Cargo Terminal
FTZ Free Trade Zone
GE   General Electric
LRP Long-range Planning
MCC Mission Core Competencies
PIMS Profit Impact Market Study
SBU Strategic Business Unit
SWOT Strengths Weaknesses Opportunities Threats
WOC Free Port Zone

1. Introduction

Background

Strategic management is a relatively young but dynamic field of research which concentrates upon improving a company's position relative to its competitive environment. New tools and techniques are continuously being tailored to match the ever-changing business environment, this time for the "new" i.e. post down-sized, post transition organisation operating in a global, fast changing, unpredictable environment. Traditional models and tools like portfolio matrices however, are still in use but in a refined way. Now that business processes have been re-engineered, researchers turn to re-engineer strategy: designing re-active real-time systems which are able to cope with continuous organisational change imposed by the acceleration of the external environment.

Poland is a country transforming from a centrally planned into a free market economy. This, together with changes in other East European countries, has caused dramatic changes in political, legal, economic, social and technological aspects over the last few years, leaving businesses struggling with a highly turbulent environment.

Polish ports do not only face severe and increasing competition in a highly turbulent and fast growing East European transport sector. As ports, they face additional problems particular to the industry: these include high investment sums as opposed to low cash-flows; long-term investment as opposed to short term changes in ship design, technology and trade patterns.

Conceptually[1], this text analyses research that can be located at the intersection of these three fields. The sub-theme of environmental turbulence

---

[1] See Appendix 1.

1

at the intersection of "strategic management" and "the Polish environment" runs as the linking factor through the study.

Methodologically, the research can be located in the area of explorative/descriptive field studies in Snow and Thomas' (1994) classification of strategic management research. Although it is theory testing by its nature, the process of observation, hypothesis building and testing, and subsequent modification ... are interrelated steps in the process of scientific enquiry (Chadwick 1981:66) so that this study's observation also contributes to the building of new scientific and exploratory frameworks.

Objectives of the study

The objectives of this study are:

(1) to analyse the process of strategy-making in the ports of Gdańsk and Gdynia, i.e. to determine its elements, their sequence, interdependence and any possible feedback loops;

(2) to examine whether there is a correlation between the strategic management system that exists, the techniques and tools currently applied and the level of environmental turbulence as perceived by the various port authorities;

(3) to analyse inter-port variations of strategic management, if any, and explain why they occur even though both ports share effectively the same location and are subject to largely the same external influences.

Hypotheses

The study tests the following three hypotheses:

(1) The ports of Gdańsk and Gdynia are expected to apply a process of strategy making where all steps of the classical model are employed in sequential order.

(2) The ports of Gdańsk and Gdynia are expected to have different strategic management systems and to apply different techniques and tools. Both ports have carried out the process of transformation and privatisation in a unique way and this is

expected to be mirrored in their approach towards strategic management as well.

(3) The two ports are expected to apply a strategic management system which is applicable for an environmental turbulence level of medium degree. Strategic management systems designed specifically for a highly turbulent environment are only now just beginning to emerge and thus are not well enough understood yet to be applied even where the context may demand that such an intensity of approach is necessary.

Relevance and limitations of the study

Strategic management, ports and the Polish transformation process are well studied subjects and there is an extensive literature on each of these areas but in particular strategic management generally and the transformation process in Poland. As a result, what can and does this research contribute new to the world?

First it aims at closing a gap - not only one gap but several:

In the field of strategic management, much of the extensive research literature as well as a considerable number of applications in industry note a sizeable gap between theory and practice and go on to urge for case studies to be carried out to generate further knowledge about issues relevant for industry.

Strategic management concepts mainly originated in manufacturing companies. As they spilled over to other industrial sectors they had to be adapted to meet the changed environment. Meanwhile, strategic management in the port industry is still in its infancy even in the west. To enable this highly competitive industry to enjoy fully the fruits of adopting an advanced and appropriate strategic management approach and structure, the most suitable models possible have to be constructed. This in turn requires further observation, experimentation and hypothesis testing.

Following the substantial changes within Eastern Europe and the globalisation of markets in general, the nature and level of environmental turbulence is currently a topical issue amongst both managers and theoretical strategists. The challenge is to refine present strategic management concepts to cope with the increasing turbulence that is bound to remain. This study aims to take Obloj and Howard's research on strategies of successful Polish firms (1996) at least one step further and extend it to the range of Polish port enterprises and authorities that exists.

Secondly, this research draws on the work of Ledger and Roe (1993 and 1996) who used conceptual modelling to analyse the impact of social, political and economic change in Eastern Europe upon the Polish shipping industry in eight (1993) and respectively ten (1996) sub-contextual matrix models. The study here, in adhering to the Ledger and Roe model, operates in particular in the managerial/organisational sub-context when it attempts to analyse which factors have a significant impact upon the design of strategic management systems; additionally, it carries the analysis over into the sector of the Polish port industry, represented by two of its major players: the ports of Gdańsk and Gdynia.

This study focuses primarily upon the process and content dimensions of strategy. It is thus limited in the sense that the very sizeable topic of strategic content has had to be excluded. This area has been and will continue to be the subject of a considerable number of studies and as a consequence, there is already a sufficient number of excellent documentations and recommendations that have been produced.[2] At the same time, since strategic content is one of the three main dimensions of strategy, it will run inevitably as an underground stream through this study, occasionally springing to the surface to make its importance and relevance clear to the argument.

The underlying premise of this study is that strategic management as such - and there is a proven record of more than 30 years for doing so - can improve company performance and can create a competitive advantage in any market place including that of the international ports industry.

Methodology

The research outlined here has employed various methods of data collection to meet the requirements of the study. Primary data were collected during a series of site visits when officials of both ports were interviewed and asked to complete a questionnaire. Those officials of the target group of ten who were not available received the questionnaire with a covering letter by mail for self-completion. Further opinion was obtained during semi-structured interviews with representatives of public bodies, academic institutions, research institutes and members of the group responsible for the privatisation process of Polish ports. To guarantee confidentiality, it was agreed that names would not be disclosed. Secondary data were gathered from port

---

[2] Tubielewicz, A. (1997). Strategy of the Gdańsk Port Authority. (in Polish); Masterplan for Port Gdańsk 1995; Tubielewicz, A. (1994). Kompleksowe zagospodarownie portu Gdańsk [Complex development of the Port of Gdańsk]. Gdańsk: Instytut Morski (in Polish); Port Sector Study Poland (1994). World Bank and RMG. Port Strategic Plan for Port of Gdynia 1993. According to Gdynia port officials a North American/Canadian strategic feasibility study will be undertaken in 1998

publications, internal documents, and governmental publications as well as from books, journals, newspapers and statistics available in the university maritime libraries of Plymouth and Cardiff in the United Kingdom and Sopot, Poland.

Overview of the study

This study is divided into seven chapters. Whilst this introductory chapter has broadly framed the purpose and focus of the research, the comprehensive literature review in the second chapter addresses the issue of strategic management. Chapter Three, introduces the ports of Gdynia and Gdańsk and then turns its attention to the Polish environment. Chapter Four contains an analysis of the conceptual models for the research and then goes on to assess the study's methodological aspects. It provides detail about the research methods adopted, the conduct of the field research and discusses a number of design issues.

The results of the study are presented in Chapter Five and will be discussed in detail in Chapter Six. The study concludes with a summary of the managerial implications of the research, a conclusion of the hypothesis testing and recommendations for future research.

2. Strategic management - a review of the literature

Introduction

This chapter provides an intensive review of the literature upon strategic management within five sections. To familiarise the reader with the subject, a beginning is made with definitions and basic concepts, introducing the three dimensions of strategy, explaining hierarchy levels and then going on to the types of strategies that exist.

A second section invites the reader for a short historical journey through the evolutionary process of the theory of strategic management. The aim is to understand how the focus of theoretical research not only changed over time, but how the tools and techniques that have been employed have become more complex and sophisticated in an attempt to capture the high complexity of the fast-changing business environment. In the next section the process of strategy making is explored in some depth: this includes consideration of mission statement, audit, strategic choice, implementation and control. Additionally, strategic management tools and techniques used in each step of the process are presented and analysed. Section four relates strategic management to the port industry and port authorities and addresses the question whether ports can benefit from this type of management and looks at the potential usage of strategic management in different business contexts. This chapter concludes by assigning each level of environmental turbulence to a specific strategic management system.

Definitions and basic concepts

Strategy defined

Strategy is of Greek origin meaning "the art of warfare" (Duden Fremdwoerterbuch 1966). As the twentieth century comes to an end and the 21st century approaches, the commercial and organisational battle is beginning to be fought on different grounds - including market share and the like - and it is now company directors who are asking the four questions of strategy:

    1) Where are we now?
    2) Where do we want to be in the future?
    3) How do we get there?
    4) How do we assure safe arrival?

Question number one is concerned with the analysis of the present state of the organisation and its environment. Question number two deals with the mission and goals of the firm. The third question is about formulating ideas concerning the set of actions that may lead to the achievement of missions and goals, evaluating the alternatives and finally choosing which one or ones that are most appropriate. The fourth question addresses the issue of implementation and control of strategies (see Fifield and Gilligan 1995:XIII). Strategies - understood in a narrower sense - can be defined as the means, or the set of actions that are or need to be taken to achieve the organisational goals of the company or authority that is under examination (Koontz 1992, David 1995).

What then is strategic management and how does it differ from other types of management?

Strategic management defined

Management is, according to Koontz and Weihrich (1990:4), the

> "process of [creating] an environment in which individuals, working together in groups, efficiently accomplish selected aims"

As such it involves passing through a number of stages including those of planning, organising, staffing, leading and control.

Strategic management, in contrast, is "at general management's core" (Porter 1996:77). It is concerned with the future, long-term impacts of current decisions made by managers who have responsibility for running the organisation as a whole (Rosen 1995:2). Or, to give a rather more negative definition from Porter (1996):

> "strategic management is not operational effectiveness. Strategic management involves choice." (Porter 1997)

This involves positioning the company so that is does things *differently* from its competitors (Porter 1996:62) and searching for an appropriate strategic fit - i.e. matching the capabilities of the firm to the environment in which it works (Johnson and Scholes 1997:4).

On the vast ocean of strategic management literature, strategic management sails on many a ship including: "business policy" (Jauch and Glueck 1988) , "corporate strategy" (Johnson and Scholes 1997), "strategic planning" (Mintzberg 1994a-d), or "strategic posture management" (Ansoff 1990). Business policy tends to focus upon internal issues and seeks to harmonise the firm's functional activities (Hunger and Wheelen 1996:5). Strategic planning and posture management are evolutionary forms of strategic management systems and as such they will be discussed in a later section in this chapter. In the context of this study, strategic management is interpreted in its widest sense encompassing the above mentioned systemic variations.

The three dimensions of strategy

It is generally[1] acknowledged that there are three dimensions[2] of strategy (Pettigrew 1988, Mintzberg 1990a) reflected in Figure 1.

Process refers to the steps an organisation proceeds through to come up with a strategy it wants to pursue; this is the *how* of the strategic management process. The output of this process is "the strategy" of the organisation. When looking at *what* set of actions is required to achieve the goals that have been set, the researchers look at the *content* of strategy. Finally, the *what* and the *how* of strategy are always connected to the firm's external and internal environment, i.e. they are always *context* related as without consideration of all environmental factors their impact is meaningless.

---

[1] A minority of researchers, like Feurer and Chaharbaghi (1995), define eight dimensions.
[2] It is appropriate to talk of dimensions rather than of elements, since they are heavily interconnected (de Wit and Meyer 1994:xi).

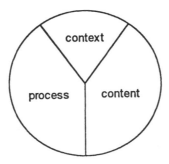

Figure 1: The three dimensions of strategy
Source: Authors

Strategic management and functions management

Strategy as such is not a stranger to financial thinking, where terms like S(trategic) B(usiness) F(inance) (Ward and Grundy 1996:321) have been used. Although strategic management on the other hand is evolving and embraces many aspects of management, financial literature sees strategic management still as essentially a form of non-financial thinking and perceives a diametrical opposition in its existence and application.[3] As regards marketing, here Piercy (1995) observes an overlap between strategic management and marketing. He advocates tearing down the demarcation line that exists between them and categorising decision making in terms of (internal or external) focus and the respective level of origin (high or low).

Hierarchy of strategy

Strategy is of an hierarchical nature. In large corporations, strategy typically can be encountered on three levels[4]: these are the corporate, (strategic) business (unit) and functional levels. Where strategy is *initiated*, however, is

---

[3] Ward and Grundy try to link the two concepts to overcome this "schizophrenic tension".
[4] "Enterprise", a fourth level, is occasionally mentioned; it deals with the wider environment, cf. Freeman and Lorange (1985).

a matter of organisational culture and management style and will be discussed in some detail in a later chapter.

Considered artificial by those who stress the aspect of interrelationship between the levels (Jauch and Gluck 1988:10, Boswell 1983), the majority of literature draws a sharp demarcation line between these levels (Hunger 1996:17-20, Johnson and Scholes 1997: de Wit and Meyer 1994). Corporate strategy is usually maintained to be concerned with:

a) the overall directions of the corporation in terms of which businesses to pursue (particularly relating to the mission); and

b) with the balancing of portfolios as well as with resource allocation. Here the choice between stability, growth or retrenchment strategies is decided.

At the divisional level, business strategy tends to be concerned with the competitive position of the particular division's product/service within its market or industry. To gain competitive advantage, overall cost leadership and differentiation strategies may be employed. Functional strategy finally, concentrates upon how to maximise performance. Strategies from the higher levels are commonly translated down into operational plans and policies.

Whether a strategy will be successful depends to a large extent upon how well the strategy levels interact. Consistent with the holistic approach of this study, the subsequent chapters focus on the strategies of the first two levels.

Development of strategy

Types of strategy: how strategy comes about

A strategy does not emerge out of the blue, it evolves. Mintzberg (as referenced in Johnson and Scholes 1997:44) was the first to classify the way

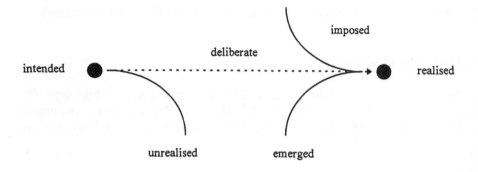

Figure 2: Strategy development routes
Source: Mintzberg and Waters (1985); Mintzberg (1984); Mintzberg and Quinn (1996)

that strategies are developed and in the process constructed the model that is outlined in Figure 2.

Intended (planned) strategy becomes (deliberately) *realised* strategy only when it is implemented and put into action. However, in business life, during the process of formulation and implementation strategy, part of the original content may be lost, thus becoming *unrealised* strategy. This may be due to intention or as a result of mistakes but in either case the result is the same. *Imposed* strategies are those which are dictated, be it by external circumstances like legal or economic conditions or by reasons rooted in the company itself. Finally, strategies may develop over time in close relation to the changing environment: if this is the case then a strategy is said to have *emerged.*

Which approach the port authorities of Gdańsk and Gdynia have and will favour will be presented in the later chapter which concentrates upon the analytical part of this study.

The process of strategy formulation in relation to time: punctuated equilibrium

The strategic direction of an organisation changes over time. Research (e.g. Mintzberg 1979) was able to identify the following patterns of strategy development which have acquired the name of punctuated equilibrium:[5]

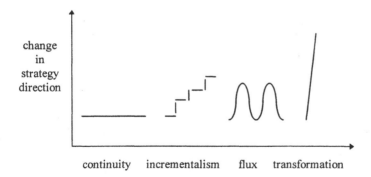

Figure 3: Punctuated equilibrium
Source: Johnson and Scholes (1997:41)

---

[5] see Romanelli and Tushmann (1994) for an explanation of this concept.

Incremental change involves adjustment of strategy to the changing environment in small steps (a process of fine tuning). It is most frequently observed in manufacturing or heavy industry although not to the exclusion of the service sector. *Transformation*, that is the process of fundamental strategic change, is overall the least likely to be found. During a period of *continuity* the current strategic direction is pursued further whilst in a time of *flux* strategy tends to change unsystematically and in a rather more chaotic manner (Johnson and Scholes 1997:41, 42).

During its life cycle a firm will typically adopt different patterns of strategy to cope with what is commonly known as *strategic drift* (see Jacobs 1997): naturally enough, in times of a crisis, any sort of transformational change is considerably more likely than during a phase of stability (Johnson and Scholes 1997:81).

Strategic patterns can also be related to the degree of environmental change that occurs. Incremental change will be the chosen route when the firm operates in a steadily changing environment and transformational change will be required in times of turbulence. Adjusting strategy in small steps enjoys the benefit of easier implementation. On the other hand, the organisation may disintegrate into reactive behaviour which, in the case of a sudden environmental change, will prove highly disadvantageous and may have terminal, or at least highly serious consequences.

Finally, a phenomenon labelled *strategic momentum* should be acknowledged (Miller and Friesen 1980). It suggests that a firm is highly likely to stick to a chosen strategic direction in the sense that new strategies will "develop from and within that strategy" instead of them performing a 180° turn (Johnson and Scholes 1997:41). Problems that emerge from this approach to strategy belong systematically to the topics of "implementation" and "managing strategic change". Therefore, it will be discussed in the corresponding section later in this text.

The evolution of strategic management

Following Feurer and Chaharbaghi (1995), the evolution of strategic management concepts took place in five distinct phases that can be readily determined from the literature. These phases are strategic planning, generalisation, strategic management, strategy process research and dynamic strategy formulation and implementation (Figure 4).

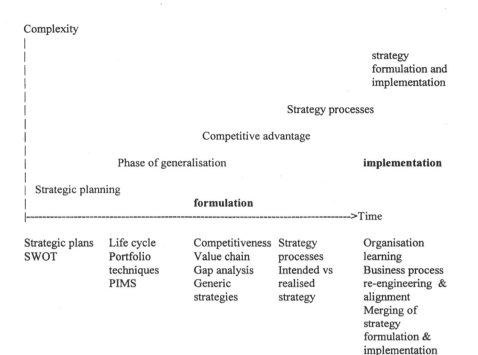

Complexity

```
|
|                                                    strategy
|                                                    formulation and
|                                                    implementation
|
|                                   Strategy processes
|
|                            Competitive advantage
|
|              Phase of generalisation              implementation
|
| Strategic planning
|                            formulation
|------------------------------------------------------------------------>Time
```

Strategic plans	Life cycle	Competitiveness	Strategy	Organisation
SWOT	Portfolio	Value chain	processes	learning
	techniques	Gap analysis	Intended vs	Business process
	PIMS	Generic	realised	re-engineering &
		strategies	strategy	alignment
				Merging of
				strategy
				formulation &
				implementation

Figure 4: The evolution of strategic management
Source: Feurer and Chaharbaghi (1995)

Phase 1: Strategic planning

Ansoff (1965) and Andrews and Christiansen (as referenced in Feurer and Chaharbaghi 1995) pioneered the new field of strategic planning in the early 1960's.[6] In doing this, they left behind the era of long-range planning (LRP) which had been characterised by a tendency towards inflexibility, where predictions for the future were made by the extrapolation of past growth and where future development fell along the same lines as those trends that had already been pursued (Ansoff and McDonnell 1990:15). In strategic planning, on the contrary, a strategy is developed by following a specific sequence of actions in the order of problem analysis, strategy generation, strategy option evaluation, choice of strategy and finally implementation (Feurer and Chaharbaghi 1995:12). In the view of others of the same design

---

[6] Strategic Planning was not confined to manufacturing industry; the first to develop a concept of strategic planning for urban and regional planning was Chadwick (1981) in 1971.

school, strategy is always concerned with matching the organisation's capabilities with the prospects that exist or are anticipated to develop in the business environment (Christensen et al. 1982). The output of strategic planning consists not only of operational goals and budgets as is the case in Long Range Planning, but also additionally a series of carefully considered and designed, strategic goals and programmes (Ansoff and McDonnell 1990:16).

However, inevitably the business environment changes with time so that the historical strengths of a firm may not be capabilities in the future but in fact can be drawbacks and weaknesses. It is here that strategic planning finds the majority of its limitations. However, in spite of this perceived (and potentially actual) lack of flexibility, strategic planning is still widely practised in the majority of business environments (Ansoff and McDonnell 1990, Feurer and Chaharbaghi 1995:12).

Phase 2: Generalisation

In order to find the source of managerial success, researchers now attempted in a second step to formulate a variety of universal frameworks. Porter suggested that successful firms tend to choose one particular strategy out of three rather more broad, generic strategies (1980, 1985). He also designed a framework to assess the attractiveness of an industry by looking at the five forces that are commonly operating within it (Porter 1985). The concept of life cycle models was introduced to help to understand the development of a product, firm and/or industry (Flamholz 1990). Researchers also invented a variety of tools to balance the allocation of resources with the product and/or service range of a company and as a consequence, portfolio techniques exemplified by the BCG matrix or the GE matrix were born.[7] As a consequence, organisational values and structures were now intensively studied (Feurer and Chaharbaghi 1995) and Chandler's (1970) findings that commonly, the organisational structure of a firm determines how strategies are generated and put into action, were finally verified.

Phase 3: Strategic management: obtaining sustainable competitive advantage

It was not long before it became apparent in the literature that these universal concepts were unable to account fully for the success of a firm. Hence, in the 1980's the era of strategic management dawned (Schendel and Hofer 1979). Research turned to attempting to lay bare the roots of sustainable competitive advantage. This term denotes the set of elements which causes a firm's

---

[7] These tools and techniques will be explained in a later section.

performance to be superior within its competitive environment on a long-term and sustainable basis (Feurer and Chaharbaghi 1995:15).

According to the resource-based school of thought (e.g. Stalk et al. 1992), competitive advantage lies in using organisational capabilities to adjust the external environment that surrounds and affects the activities of the organisation. This is what is commonly termed an "inside-out" approach. The positioning school led by Porter takes the view that the firm has to adapt to the environment within which it is working to have any hope of being successful, thus maintaining what they term an "outside-in" perspective (de Wit and Meyer 1994:215). Others found that the implementation of strategy can constitute a major source of competitive advantage within the marketplace and created tools characterised by the "value chain" and McKinsey's "7 S" (Engelhoff 1993). Quality and time were identified as two further factors of influence along with the ability to be innovative and to adapt into what was termed as a "learning organisation" (Meyer 1993; Stalk and Hout 1990, Martinsons 1993, Senge 1990).

Phase 4: Era of strategy process research

In a second step, researchers discovered the importance of the process of strategy in the firm's struggle to obtain a *sustainable* competitive advantage. Many, mostly incompatible, typologies[8] were developed amongst which Mintzberg's and Miles and Snow's (1978) attempts in this area, are the best known.

Phase 5: Dynamic strategy formulation and implementation

Today both researchers and those working in the industry include the acceleration of environmental change within their models. They acknowledge the Ashby theorem of requisite variety and argue that continuous external change must be mirrored and matched by continuous internal change if a company wants to be successful in the long term. This implies a process of continuous change of strategic content and process. At the same time, internal change has to be so rapid in order to match the high-speed environmental changes that occur, that the steps of formulation and implementation have a tendency to melt down into one single process. Since the outcome of the environmental change is usually unknown, strategies cannot be planned firmly but are subject to continuous innovation. As a consequence, so it is argued, innovative potential will be at the highest level when the whole organisation is involved in formulating and implementing

---

[8] see Feurer and Chaharbaghi (1995:18) for a selection of strategy process models.

the strategic process. The concept of "learning organisations" has returned again (Senge 1990,1994).

As a result research tends currently to focus upon "maximising change potential". Various approaches are regularly undertaken[9]. Although they differ in style and content, in their essence they all stress the need for a dynamic approach to strategy (Feurer and Chaharbaghi 1995). Interestingly enough, at the same time, the term "strategic planning" is beginning to be rejuvenated.[10]

In conclusion it can be said that strategic management takes a variety of approaches. Theory has progressed from a static, structured, simple planning attitude towards one that is dynamic and creative in its approach, employing a series of sophisticated tools and stressing that the whole organisation has to be involved in order to create vital drive from within, which is needed to maximise change potential and to meet the environmental pressures that come from without. Industry in general employs all the approaches we have noted here but the older and more traditional concepts tend to be better known as one would anticipate (Ansoff 1990:12). In later sections in this book, in Chapters Five and Six, we will analyse which of the approaches if any, is taken by the port authorities of Gdañsk and Gdynia within the dynamically changing environment of Poland's port industry.

The process of strategy-making

Overview

Models of the strategy process differ in the number and the variety of names used for their elements: some have three, others four or more elements. Glueck and Jauch (1988) as well as Johnson and Scholes (1997), for example, favour "strategic analysis", "choice" and "implementation". David (1995) uses "formulation", "implementation" and "evaluation". Rosen (1995:130) arranges six elements of the strategy process like a string of pearls and disregards implementation and control issues because he considers them elements of strategic management rather than of the strategic process.

Nevertheless, there is a general consensus that the process of strategy-making consists of a series of elements comprising a mission statement, (both an external and internal) audit, the generation of strategic alternatives, their evaluation and choice and finally, their implementation and control.

---

[9] see Feurer and Chaharbaghi (1995:18) for an overview.
[10] Mintzberg, H. (1994a).The fall and rise of strategic planning; Mintzberg, H. (1994c, d). Rethinking strategic planning; part I and II; Wilson, I. (1994). Strategic planning isn't dead - it changed.

These elements are not necessarily in sequential order but they are always interrelated (Moore 1995). Also, they will differ from one firm to another in their importance. This variety in influence will be explained in more detail in a later section. It is only for convenience in structuring this topic, that this study has followed a sequential model which is outlined in Figure 5 and which is a form that is common to other research studies in this broad area described in the literature.

The process of strategy-making

Mission

A logical starting point for crafting a new strategy or reviewing an existing one is the ubiquitous mission statement (Rosen 1995:131). A mission statement should answer the question "What is our business?" (Drucker 1974:61). It is a statement of intent (Bowman and Asch 1996:100) of what the firm wants to be, its broad goals, the culture it strives to engender and its values. It is the cultural glue (Campbell el. al. 1990). Mission statements may come disguised as "statement of purpose", "value statement", "goal" or "corporate philosophy" (Leuthesser 1997). They should not become confused with vision statements which ask "What do we want to become?" (David 1995:91). A wide range of research has shown[11] that mission statements may be made up of various elements which include the naming of customers, the service/products involved, the relevant geographical domain, the desired image, the company's self concept and philosophy, the core technologies that it will apply and/or the profitability goals of the organisation.

Mission statements are quite commonly concise and very brief but on the other hand they may also appear as what are sometimes known as "theme" statements where the elements of the mission are effectively embedded within a storylike framework (Leuthesser 1997).

Audit

In order to be able to respond to or even to anticipate a changing environment, the organisation must first fully monitor and analyse the environment over a reasonably long period of time (Rosen 1995). It then must analyse the internal situation before finding what it hopes to be a suitable and appropriate strategic fit.

---

[11] see Leuthesser (1997) and David (1995).

External audit

When applied to the ports industry, the firm (a port) operates within a recognisable market, namely the maritime transport market. It belongs to the port industry, but may also operate within a number of other markets, for example fruit retailing (as the Port of Gdynia does) or the hotel sector, as does the Port of Singapore. In addition, other industries (in this case those characterised by road and rail transport for example) will also be operating in the firm's prime market. However, the firm (port) could also define itself as being part of an industry who's prime purpose is adding-value-to-customer activity. To provide an example of this, Figure 6 illustrates the firm in its macro-environment.

In the case where adding value is the central issue, the firm's markets and its industrial context would be very different. It follows that "defining the business the firm is in" (through the mission statement) can be of crucial importance and may well indeed influence further stages in the strategy process.

An analysis of the external environment will be undertaken by looking at the industry, the market place and finally, the macro-environment. This sequence is depicted in Figure 7. For an analysis of the industry, Porter's "Five Forces Model" as outlined in Appendix 3 is often applied. The aim of this model is to gain an understanding of the forces which are operating within the specific industry and to assess the industry's profitability (Porter 1980). Porter uses the concepts of "bargaining power of suppliers", "competitive rivalry", "bargaining power of customers", "threats of substitutes and alternatives" and "barriers to entry" as characteristics. This model can also be used on the next level of analysis, the market place (see Rosen 1995:38).

To understand the macro-environment, PEST-analysis (or sometimes called STEP-analysis) provides help by analysing trends in the political, economic, socio-cultural and technological macro-sphere of the organisation.

Internal audit

Aspects of internal audit. The next step in the process of strategy analysis is to evaluate the internal situation of the company since a chosen strategy must be in line with the strategic capabilities of the firm (Johnson and Scholes 1997:137). Traditionally four aspects have been considered: those of financial performance, company functions, the structure of the organisation and the cultural web which permeates the activities of the company and has impacts upon its strategic capabilities (Rosen 1995:47).

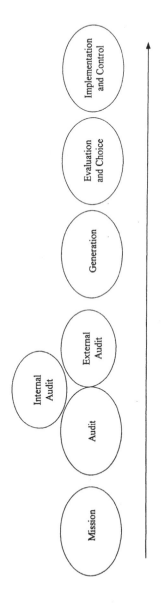

Figure 5: The process of strategy making
Source: adapted from Rosen (1994), David (1995)

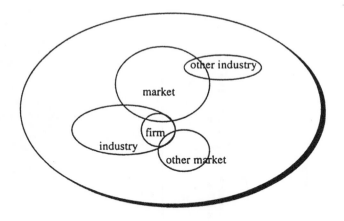

Figure 6: The firm in its macro-environment
Source: Rosen (1995:43)

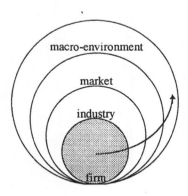

Figure 7: Analysis of the environment
Source : Authors

The concept of financial performance will not be subject to review in this study since access to internal financial statistics is rather difficult for outside investigators to achieve with any level of realism and thus with any true value This should not suggest it is not a valuable activity in strategic terms if it can be achieved at a rigorous level. As a consequence, this point will not be elaborated upon further. Meanwhile, a functional analysis attempts to look at how the functions (those of finance, marketing and operations) are performing within the organisation. A structural analysis investigates whether the firm is set up in accordance with these functions, according to its products/services (divisional) or whether it combines line and staff functions (matrix) together.

Organisational behaviour is characterised by the firm's culture, its power and leadership. Leadership can be democratic, where decisions are made in a top-down/bottom-up exchange of levels. It can also be autocratic, applying top-down control. Adhocracies are characterised by non-systemic, creative behaviour (Mintzberg and Quinn 1996). Culture denotes the common set of traditions and values particular to the firm in question.

Apart from applying these internal measures, a company's internal strength must also be evaluated in relation to its environmental context. This is commonly achieved through the application of portfolio analysis.

Portfolio techniques

Portfolio analysis is most typically undertaken at a corporate level. It originated in the 1970s when a large number of manufacturing industries started to produce many products for many markets, and corporations were suddenly faced with the decision how their resources should be allocated between the differing demands that emerged. Portfolio analysis' underlying rationale is that the long and short-term profits of the elements and their interdependence within the portfolio should be recognised within a strategic approach (Fifield and Gilligan 1995:95).

Portfolio models all plot the position of Strategic Business Units (SBUs) in matrices. However, they all differ in the variables and the grade of scaling used to assess SBUs. Appendix 2 provides some detailed explanation of the BCG and McKinsey/GE matrices. The use of portfolio techniques is made easy since a simple strategic action can be prescribed for each matrix-segment. Although each company may and in fact will have preferences as to how the elements should be positioned in order to obtain a balanced portfolio, the portfolio techniques nevertheless leave enough manoeuvrability for just that to be achieved.

As with any model, the degree of validity strongly depends upon the quality and quantity of the input data (Fifield and Gilligan 1995). Later developed models such as the McKinsey/GE matrix tried to include a larger number of environmental factors but critics still argue that the real environment cannot be adequately reflected (Johnson and Scholes 1997). Therefore a series of new models are still being devised and adapted.[12] That portfolio techniques provide just a snapshot of the present situation and therefore have a tendency towards becoming too static can easily be circumvented by drawing several matrices for a variety of different points of time (Sokol: 1992).

Further explanation of Nicholls' M(ission) C(ore) C(ompetencies) matrix is needed at this stage. It blends extremely well with modern strategic thinking which largely takes a holistic view, acknowledging the importance of values and vision as reflected in the mission statement (Campbell et. al. 1990) as well as the core competencies (Tampoe 1994 as referenced in Nicholls 1995) (Figure 8).

In the MCC matrix, resource claims are not allocated according to the size of the "fruits of the organisational tree". Rather, they are plotted in a matrix according to their compliance with the organisation's strategic mission and core competencies. Drains should be discarded; drives cherished; distractions and dilutions should be converted into a drive - either by developing the product to achieve a better fit or by adjusting the framework instead (!). Thus, every time a claim is located on the grid, the strategic parameters against which the claim is tested are challenged and re-assessed at the same time. This should result in superior strategy. Another distinct advantage of the MCC matrix is that not only those claims regarding products

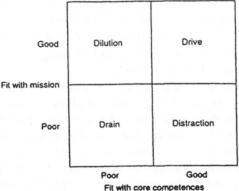

Figure 8: MCC matrix
Source: Nicholls (1995:6)

---

[12] for example the M(ission)C(ore)C(ompetencies) Matrix.

but any claim upon resources can be assessed. Finally, the MCC matrix can be employed at any strategic level. For those managers who prefer directional policy matrices, Nicholls provides an MCC version which is illustrated at the end of this text in Appendix 2. In conclusion it can be agreed with Grant (1995:412) that portfolio matrices may be simplistic, but their ability to reflect all the business activities of an organisation at one glance is powerful.

Generating strategies

Having assessed the external environment and the internal capabilities of the organisation, the strategist will now go on to generate strategic alternatives. David (1995) distinguishes 13 basic alternative strategies, each of which has various sub-alternatives plus the three generic strategies developed by Porter. Johnson and Scholes (1997) maintain that there are three generic i.e. fundamental strategies, which provide the basis for strategy-making. These are defined as cost leadership, differentiation and focus. A firm can then set off in different directions, namely they can undertake "withdrawal", "consolidation" or "diversification" or follow one of Ansoff's four development strategies. The firm can use three alternative methods to pursue its goal these constituting internal development, acquisition or joint development.

Porter (1980, 1985) was the first to link superior performance of a firm with the type of strategy it pursued. His original framework is illustrated in Appendix 4. In his view a firm must choose between one of the three strategies that he outlines. Those who find themselves getting "stuck in the middle" will not be able to gain sustainable competitive advantage over other organisations in the marketplace.

His concept of mutual exclusiveness is currently being challenged since it has been discovered that "relationship" and "co-operation" not only with customers, but also with competitors, are new and valid strategies which can lead to a competitive advantage. The idea of forming alliances is well demonstrated by the liner shipping industry for example. For the ship management industry, this phenomenon was recently analysed by Gray and Panayides (1997) for a variety of ship management companies. As regards the liner industry the formation of alliances is well practised and has now been refined in the development of liner consortia.

As a recognition of the clear and emerging shortcomings of Porter's model, the "strategy clock" was developed (Johnson and Scholes 1997:253). It categorises generic strategies in terms of price and perceived added value for the customer and provides relatively easy evaluation of the situation. It is illustrated in Appendix 4 with some additional interpretation of how the technique can be used.

To generate strategic ideas the SWOT analysis can also be used. In a matrix the organisational strengths and weaknesses are listed against environmental (external) threats and opportunities. The most favourable strategy is usually found to be to use internal strengths to exploit external opportunities. An outline of the SWOT model application can be found in Appendix 5.

Evaluation and choice

To be able to evaluate a strategic alternative, some sort of yardstick is needed. It is in this step that mission, values, goals, the organisational culture and the leadership style make their most significant impact upon the success or otherwise of the organisation.

Evaluation criteria are suitability, feasibility and acceptability to stakeholders (Johnson and Scholes 1997:21). Suitability stands for searching the strategic fit, that is finding a strategy which fits to the organisation as well as to the external environment. Feasibility denotes the extent to which the strategy can be put into action. Stakeholders are all those upon whom the firm depends to carry out its task and vice versa (Johnson and Scholes 1997:196) e.g. shareholders, customers, employees ... Evaluation and choice will also be undertaken in the light of implementability. In a trade-off, a firm may chose a strategy with lower quality but higher level of implementability (Bowman and Asch 1996:99).

The final choice typically will be made in a number of steps, where the first stage will include the setting up of a shortlist. These options will then be evaluated by the weighting of alternatives or, in a less sophisticated strategy, simply by comparing the advantages and disadvantages that exist for alternative strategies (Rosen 1995).

Implementation and control

The final step in the process model is that of implementation and control. Implementation is concerned with putting strategies into action (McNamee 1992:11, Johnson and Scholes 1993:16). Control deals with the question of whether the chosen strategy brings the organisation closer to where it wants to be some time in the future.

Control can be undertaken through;

a) review of operational results;
b) review of strategic content, i.e. the chosen strategy;
c) review of the process of strategy-making, i.e. how strategies are derived; or
d) review of the control system, i.e. what is measured by the control mechanism that is in place.

How implementation and control are undertaken in an organisation depends strongly upon its structure, the styles of control that exist and the organisational culture (Rosen 1995). A centralised organisation has different methods and approaches to an organisation where divisions are largely independent.

One main area of concern remains the management of strategic change (Johnson and Scholes 1997). It was discussed in an earlier chapter that strategies develop a momentum which causes the increase of resistance to change. Research has shown that organisations are characterised by hard (strategy, structure, systems) and soft (style, skills, staffing, shared values) elements. The "7 S" framework which is illustrated in Appendix 6 is a model which supports such an approach. Ansoff and McDonnell (1990) identify two types of resistance within an organisation; behavioural resistance by individuals or groups, and systematic resistance by active opposition or passive incompetence.

The future desired feature of the organisation is indicated by the dotted line, whilst the present state of the firm is represented by the solid line. Forces in the figure which propel the organisation towards its goals are pushing forces.

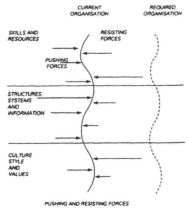

Figure 9: Force field approach
Source: Bowman and Asch (1996:115), Faulkner and Bowman (1995:123)

25

Resisting forces are those which pose barriers to change. However, it is only when resistance to change is detected that it can be minimised. - and this is a prerequisite for successful strategy translation. Blockages to change can be identified by using (for example) the instrument of force field analysis as illustrated in Figure 9.

Number and choice of strategic tools

This chapter has presented a myriad of strategic management tools which have been created and developed by researchers. It has to be stressed that the choice of tools has a direct impact upon the implementability and the general success of strategy that is chosen. Meanwhile, the question arises of how many and which set of tools should a firm employ? Whilst literature treats the advantages and disadvantages of single tools in depth, this crucial issue, surprisingly, has been rarely addressed despite its clear significance for the success or otherwise of an organisation.

First of all it should be noted that there is no one-and-only perfect mix. Rather, the choice will have to be made in accordance with each company's actual situation and circumstances. However, Sokol (1992) provides a framework advocating "simplified strategic planning" (Table 1).

Simplified Strategic Planning		
Number of Tools	Tool-mix Criteria	
	The tools should ...	rather than ...
few core tools: +/- 5	provide analysis and synthesis	analysis only
	reflect dynamics in environment	statics
	provide long-term general outlook	short-term details
	provide a cross-selection of different tool groups	belong to one group only

Table 1: Simplified strategic planning
Source: Authors

Number of tools

As summarised in Table 1, a focus upon a few, i.e. possibly only +/- 5 core tools selected from a list of eleven core tools, avoids overlaps and inconsistency in their application. This will result in a simplified process which in turn is likely to increase relevance, comprehensibility and implementability of strategic decisions that are eventually made within the organisational structure.

Core tools are considered to be[13]:

product life cycle	critical success factors
competitive analysis	value chain analysis
stakeholder analysis	framework
product/market analysis	financial models
portfolio classification	gap analysis
operating budgets	

Determination of the appropriate tool-mix

The first step is the definition of the problem(s) which are to be solved. Then a choice amongst core tools will be made following these guidelines:

Step 1: Choose tools for achieving both analysis and synthesis. Following Mintzberg's model, strategy consists of both aspects and this dualism should be mirrored in the selection of tools. Tools of synthesis "combine ideas ... in a holistic ... way" (Sokol: 1992: 14). Examples are brainstorming and committee sessions. They can be employed in each of the stages of business definition, goal setting and strategic fit.

Step 2: Select tools for every stage of the strategy process. After having eliminated those tools which are in essence non-strategic, i.e. short-term and detail orientated, a set of tools should be selected that covers all stages of the strategy process.[14] A tool-mix of, for example, product life cycle, experience curve and portfolio matrixes where market share and cash flow are the analysed variables, would create overlap and should be swapped for a more effective set.

Step 3: Highlight the changing dynamics of the business over time. Finally, changes in key dynamic factors like economy, organisational issues

---

[13] Eyebrows may rise since SWOT is not included although it is heavily used in practice and highly praised by the literature

[14] Sokol defines here six groups in correspondence with his six steps of the planning process. His model differs from the approach undertaken by this paper. Therefore the way tools are grouped as such is not as important as the idea to use tools throughout the strategy process.

or competition should be captured by using dynamic tools such as product cycle models, comparative analysis or financial simulations. Alternatively, static tools could be adapted to attempt to include this feature although this will almost inevitably be a sub-optimal solution.

Strategic management and ports

"Almost no port does strategic planning but every port plans strategically". (AAPA 1988)

Port Development International, The Port and Harbour Authority and other journals and periodicals available for port managers frequently feature strategy, but rarely contain anything that implies strategic content and context. The art of strategic management as such and the topic of strategic process are hardly mentioned at all. This may be surprising since similar features are regularly found in journals of the related transport and in particular, logistics industries. Are port managers born strategists? Or is strategic management simply a managerial discipline which suffers from hydrophobia?

According to Frankel (1989) ports are at present subject to bigger commercial risks than ever before: long-term investments as opposed to short/term changes in ship design, technological changes and requirements, trade pattern mutation, and the seeming inevitability of high investment sums as opposed to low cash-flows. Therefore, he concludes, it is important to evaluate risks and alternatives intelligently - and thus introduce strategic planning (1989:123).

Chasan and Thomas reported positively upon the first attempts of North American ports to apply an early form of strategic management in the 1980's. In their opinion strategic planning provides "a tool for distinguishing between solid opportunities and latent disaster, and a rationale for saying no" (1988:251).

One year earlier, Arlt (1987) investigated the information requirements of the introduction of strategic planning in the port industry. He understood strategic planning as "a comprehensive basis for guiding ... the planning activities of the firm" (1987:51) and saw it as a formal approach within an organisation.

The strategic process consisted for him of a number of stages including: - corporate objective setting, the formulation of strategy, strategy implementation and strategy control.

In the remainder of his article Arlt undertakes a detailed analysis of the factors that influence the future of any chosen port. However, in general Arlt takes a mechanistic view which rather concentrates upon the operational details. Like the two approaches reviewed above, his strategic approach belongs as well to the earliest group of strategic management systems as described in an earlier section and possibly reflects a level of immaturity as a result.

In the same year as Chasan and Thomas' study, the American Association of Port Authorities (AAPA) issued a booklet to "provide to the port industry an introduction ... to the strategic planning process" (1988: foreword). Its philosophy, again, is that of earlier concepts of strategic management, namely it concentrates upon strategic planning rather than any other aspect of the process.

In 1993 the United Nations published a report after having studied a wide range of examples of strategic planning in ports. The empirical findings are still presented in the manner of a framework of strategic planning, referring to Jauch and Glueck's models. However, it is the first time that ideas of competitive advantage find their place in the literature on strategic management in ports and thus reflects some development of mature ideas in this sector.

Strategic management in ports however, is not purely an idea that is placed down upon paper. Looking at leading ports like the Port of Singapore[15] or Rotterdam, one will find that these organisations actively use mission statements[16] and other tools of strategic management to enhance their corporate activities.

Following the general insight of strategists that organisational structure is an important factor contributing to achieving competitive advantage, Thomas (1994) questions the common belief that changing the ownership structure of ports is *the* sole way to improve efficiency an issue of particular relevance in the context of change in the Polish ports sector. He maintains rather, that change of organisational structure and management culture are the key factors and that ownership alone can never be the sole determinant of achieving greater corporate success through strategy.

In conclusion it can be said that strategic management in its form of strategic planning or strategic capability management is beginning to make its entry into the port industry. Whereas most of the industry leaders are already operating on advanced strategic levels, many others are just about to incorporate it into their management techniques and thus change their approach to the marketplace.

---

[15] The Port of Singapore pursues the full privatisation of the port as a matter of strategy.

[16] see the www home-page of the Port of Singapore; Rotterdam coined the phrase "mainport"; Le Havre promotes its future features under "Port 2000 project".

Strategic management in different contexts

Having demonstrated that strategic management is applicable in the port industry as such, we will now discuss which impact the *business type* has on the elements that make up strategic management.

Strategic management and public non profit-making organisations

The Polish 1996 Port Act stipulates that the port authorities are non profit making enterprises (Kuzma 1996). However, even for such organisations the concepts of strategic management still hold good (Johnson and Scholes 1997:33, Drucker 1989, Hunger and Wheelen 1996:385-397) although with the implication that resource efficiency inevitably will be more important than service effectiveness since the relevant funding bodies will always be highly influential stakeholders.

Strategic management and privatised enterprises

It is widely recognised that privatisation forces management to become more market orientated and develop competitive strategy. Formal planning systems may continue to prevail, but in order to now communicate "public accountability" to the external environment (Johnson and Scholes 1997:32).

Chapter Six will attempt to analyse how privatisation in the ports of Gdynia and Gdańsk has so far actually changed the organisation of management structure, and the process and the importance of individual aspects of strategy development.

Strategic management, service organisations and public enterprises

Ports are also organisations providing services. In this industry sector strategic management is applicable as well (Boyle 1991). The same holds true for enterprises owned by the state or the municipality exemplified by municipal or state owned ports. Certainly, strategists in those organisations will find that mission statements, organisation goals as well as the strategies which have been adopted are subject to substantial and unavoidable political influence. As a result of this, the scope for change may be little (David 1995:73).

Strategic management systems in relation to the level of environmental turbulence

We have examined in an earlier section the potential elements of a strategic process. It was pointed out that the strategic management process consists of several interrelated but not necessarily sequential elements and that it was for the purpose of presentation only that a sequential approach was chosen. We also examined briefly the weighting of these elements in relation to the organisation's business type. Having done so, it is the next logical step to assemble the parts as a whole and look at strategic management systems.

Whereas the earlier section demonstrated that the evolution of these systems was driven by an increasing speed of change in the environment, this section focuses on the question of which strategic management system is suitable and at what level of environmental change. In order to do that, measures to assess the degree of environmental change have to be established first.

Measuring the turbulence of the environment

That the environment is becoming increasingly turbulent is common knowledge both in research as well as practitioners' cycles. Literature deals with this issue mainly when it discusses the development of strategy in relation to strategic drift. Nevertheless, these discussions tend to take place more on the level of strategic content than concentrating upon that of strategic management systems.

The increasing speed of environmental change is also a major argument in the fierce[17] academic warfare between the design-school and the "incrementalists". The proponents of the former argue that by the time a strategy has evolved incrementally the turbulent environment has already changed further thus leaving the organically developed strategy outdated. However, measures to show the degree of turbulence are hardly ever provided.

Ansoff and McDonnell (1990) and Rosen (1995) assess the level of environmental turbulence with the two measures of "changeability" and

---

[17] see meanwhile, the classic exchange of thoughts in the *Strategic Management Journal* by Mintzberg, H. (1990b). The Design School, March, pp. 171-195; Ansoff, H. I. (1991). Critique of Mintzberg's The Design School, September, pp. 449-461; Mintzberg, H. (1991). Learning 1, Planning 0., September, pp. 463-466.

"predictability", both of which have two elements: [18]

> *Changeability*
> Complexity
> Novelty
>
> *Predictability*
> Rapidity of Change
> Visibility of the Future

Complexity refers to the number of factors involved; *novelty* points to the question whether the present circumstances were encountered before. *Rapidity of change* assesses how fast the environment changes in relation to the organisation's response time. *Visibility*, finally, is concerned with adequacy and timeliness of data about the future. Ansoff suggests a turbulence scale from 1 to 5 which was also applied in the questionnaire used later in this text and applied to the ports of Gdañsk and Gdynia.

Relating strategic management systems to the degree of turbulence

Research results confirmed meanwhile that a company's achievement potential is highest when its strategy system matches the level of environmental turbulence that exists (Ansoff 1990).

Rosen (1995:121) suggests that moderate turbulence may be dealt with successfully in a variety of ways for example, by using special forecasting techniques, applying contingency plans, creating organisational complexity and obtaining experience from others, i.e. on the character and detail of tools and techniques. For highly turbulent environments he recommends substituting the traditional means-ends strategic system with "strategic issue management" and "crisis management".

Hunger and Wheelen (1996:84) maintain that a company has four choices in terms of reaction to the environment:

> to avoid, i.e. leave corporation and environment unchanged
> to influence, i.e. leave corporation unchanged but change environment
> to react, i.e. change corporation but leave environment unchanged
> to anticipate, i.e. change corporation and environment.

---

[18] Following Rosen (1995), the questionnaire arranged the four measures in three groups, combining "rapidity of change" and "visibility" in "unpredictability". This was done as a simplification step for the respondent as described in the methodology chapter.

Only the last option is considered as "strategic management". That Hunger and Wheelen talk of "changing the way the firm operates" (1996:85) may indicate that they think of a system which Ansoff (1990) refers to as "strategic posture management" located at 3.5 of his turbulence scale.

Ansoff's turbulence scale rates environmental turbulence from 1 (stable/repetitive) to 5 (creative/surprising). Level 1 hardly ever exists in free market economies. Level 5 is observed when the future brings unpredictable surprises and the familiarity of events is "discontinuous novel" - this is a level that may well have been appropriate for the Polish ports sector around 1990, following the political, economic and social changes of that period and which was particularly traumatic as it followed 40 years of Level 1. Figure 10 is self-explanatory and shows how each level can be distinguished by the four characteristics.

When Ansoff talks of rapidity of change being either slower, comparable or faster than response, he refers to the response of the firm.

	Environmental turbulence	Repetitive	Expanding	Changing	Discontinuous	Surprising
Changeability	Complexity	National Economic	+	Regional Technological	+	Global Socio-political
	Familiarity of events	Familiar	Extrapolable		Discontinuous Familiar	Discontinuous Novel
Predictability	Rapidity of change	Slower than response		Comparable to response		Faster than response
	Visibility of future	Recurring	Forecastable	Predictable	Partially predictable	Unpredictable surprises
	Turbulence level	1	2	3	4	5

Figure 10: Turbulence scale
Source: Ansoff (1990:31).

Discussion in an earlier section has already shown that the development of strategic management systems was responsive to the acceleration of environmental change. Ansoff relates each management system to a specific level of his environmental turbulence scale.

Consistent with the synopsis outlined earlier, to start with the systems developed after the 1960s, strategic planning is located at 3.2 of the scale, strategic (posture) management at 3.5, strategic issue management at 4 and surprise management at 4.4.

Strategic planning differs from earlier long-range planning in that it consists additionally of a strategic control loop (Ansoff, 1990). Long-range planning uses only operating control. *Strategic posture management* is a system that, in addition to strategic planning, undertakes capabilities planning and manages resistance to change. Firms practising (real-time) *strategic issue management* continuously monitor the external environment, determine the impact and the urgency of the changes and deal with them accordingly. High-impact, highly urgent matters are dealt with immediately. Medium-impact issues are dealt with in the regular planning cycle. Low-impact issues are monitored further. Changes without impact at all are disregarded. *Strategic surprise management* will be used when the environment is so turbulent that previous plans do not apply any more. In those situations emergency responses are required. Perry et al. (1993) introduce a system on even a higher level which they call *strategic improvising*. It is characterised by an interactive nature, it fosters continuous change and is to be understood as a guidance, not a control system (1993:39-40). This type of strategic approach may well have been applicable in Poland (and even moreso in much of the rest of Eastern Europe) in the early 1990s.

Ansoff suggests that positioning systems will work effectively at turbulence levels up to a degree of 3. However, as soon as the firm enters a higher level, Ansoff (1990:24) suggests to top it up with a real-time system since the latter does not impair the system that is being used.

Summary

Strategic management is concerned with the long-term impacts on the firm of current decisions by managers; it has evolved over time, driven by the acceleration of environmental change. Its development followed a coherent logic from static-reactive to dynamic-proactive systems. Successive systems with their tools and techniques have to be understood not so much as replacements but as refinements.

The strategy process consists of elements of analysis, generation, evaluation and choice of strategic alternatives and implementation and control. These elements are interrelated, may be undertaken in a sequence and they are - depending upon the particular business type - more or less important.

Strategic management is not confined to manufacturing companies where it originated. Any organisation, even ports, can benefit from an optimised capability potential and sustainable competitive advantage.

3. The ports of Gdynia and Gdańsk

Introduction

This chapter introduces the ports of Gdynia and Gdańsk and places them in their geographical setting. It provides a brief historical background and progresses to describe their organisational and operational characteristics. It concludes with a description of the characteristics of the Polish environment with particular reference to the process of privatisation - or perhaps rather more accurately described as transformation - and the policy centred upon the free market economy which has introduced competition to the country.

The dualism of the Ports of Gdynia and Gdańsk

The ports of Gdynia and Gdańsk are located in the eastern third of the Polish coastline, only 32 km apart, Gdynia being a coastal seaport, whilst Gdańsk is largely an inland seaport although with recent developments concentrated closer to the open sea. This dualism was the result of an economic reaction to the events of history. Danzig, the old port of Poland, became the port of the Prussian enclave after the second partition of Poland. It moved on to become a "free port" in the inter-war period (Hall 1992:101) as laid down in the Versailles peace treaty of 1919, although increasingly dominated by German interests. Poland, on the other hand, re-emerged with extended boundaries and when the then city and port authorities of Danzig declined the Polish requests to use the port facilities, Poland built a new port for the nation in

Gdynia (Taylor 1984:228). Today, Gdynia and Gdańsk are together with Szczecin-Świnoujście in the west, the three largest ports of Poland.

Introduction to the Port of Gdynia

The Port of Gdynia is celebrating its 75th year of operation in 1997. Poland's main general cargo and container port has undergone tremendous structural changes, the most recent one being caused by the process of privatisation which has followed the dramatic political, economic and social changes that occurred in the late 1980s and the early 1990s.

Organisational structure

The present organisational structure of the Port of Gdynia Holding Joint Stock Company is illustrated in Appendix 8 derived from the work of Kuzma (1996). Five functional departments and the managing board are supervised by a supervisory body whilst several committees subordinate to the managing board perform advisory tasks. As a result of the process of transformation and restructuring, which will be discussed in detail in a later section, seven independent port operating companies have been formed between 1994 and 1997.

These seven subsidiaries are fully owned by the port authority which, in turn, was fully owned by the state but which is now in the process of partial transfer to other organisations. The Port Gdynia Holding holds shares[1] in a number of other, in some cases, non-port related enterprises including for example liner ship operator Baltic Container Lines, Spedcont freight rail services, the Ustka Shipyard, The Bank of Gdynia, the World Trade Center Gdynia and the Ermlaender Fruit Company.

Commodity handling and operational characteristics

The Port of Gdynia is a universal harbour in that it aims to encompass all port related activities without exception. At present it is attempting to strengthen its dominant position as the major container port in Poland and to increase its market share in handling imported cars. It also aims at becoming *the* partner for handling imported exotic fruit. It has made sizeable investments recently and during 1997, a new gas terminal and a Norwegian cement terminal have been put into use. A new ro-ro ramp was to start

---

[1] The port authority uses the term "strategic interest" (Port of Gdynia Handbook 1996).

operation in September 1997. Additionally important is the Stena Line ferry link to Karlskrona in Sweden and from 1998 onwards a Scandinavian cruise liner will call regularly at Gdynia as well. At the Swedish wharf a 1.5 ha artificial fertiliser handling terminal will be set up by the Polish company Baltic Baza Masowa over the following year, owned by the port authority and Zaklady Azotowe Pulawy (*The Coastal Times* 1997).

Total port turnover has been decreasing since 1990 from 9967 kt to 7633 kt in 1995; Polish foreign trade turnover still accounts for more than 90% of the total. Whereas ore and grain turnover declined sharply, containerised general cargo turnover had increased by around 30% in the same period. Meanwhile turnover in general cargo has again reached the level of 1990 (Appendix 9). Details which can be found in Appendix 12 illustrate that in terms of weight, general cargo and coal were the major cargoes in 1995 (Gdańsk Pomerania Development Agency 1996). Meanwhile figures for 1997 reflect a considerable increase in the volume of cargo handled particularly over 1996, with a rise of some 17% in the first six months of the year. Both oil imports and grain handling were the major causes of the growth.

The Baltic Container Terminal (BCT)

Opened on 29 October 1979, the Baltic Container Terminal (BCT) subsequently became a joint stock company in 1994. Currently, the Port Authority is sole stockholder which is supposed to change with progressing privatisation. The 50 ha BCT sees itself as "Poland's leading provider of complex services of container turnover" (BCT 1996 and 1997). It also operates a ferry passenger terminal with a capacity of 2,000 passengers/hr whilst conventional load on/load off handling started in 1980. In its present operational configuration the annual handling capacity amounts to around 250,000 TEU although lower estimates have been given as 170,000 TEU.

The Helskie-I quay, with a length of 800 m., can accommodate simultaneously up to one roll on/roll off and four load on/load off vessels with a draft less than 10m. Helskie-II, which is 178m long, serves ferries and roll on/roll off vessels with a draft of up to 8m. Two roll on/roll off vessels and three load on/load off vessels can be serviced simultaneously with a maximum of 900 TEU and 1,200 TEU respectively. For containers, the first cargo-handling storage area is 9,000 TEU. Up to 15,000 tonnes of general cargo can be stored in a 20,000 sqm warehouse area. Furthermore, a bonded area for general cargo (3,000 sqm), cars (15,000) and containers (240 TEU) is provided. Railway loading/unloading is also possible utilising a six track facility. Statistics show (Appendix 10) that turnover in the ferry as well as in the container terminal has been growing steadily since 1994, reaching new heights every year.

Overall the Baltic Container Terminal is by far the biggest container terminal in Poland and in 1995 saw some 140,000 TEU passing through. This rose to around 160,000 in 1996 and is anticipated to rise again in 1997. Due to the constrained nature of the site - it is surrounded by the city of Gdynia - and the growth in container traffic, capacity will soon be reached and there is an urgent need to develop new facilities elsewhere including taking over some land from the Naval Base adjacent. Various plans exist, but the eventual result may well be the growth of a new terminal in Gdańsk.

BCT is in effect, a feeder port with regular links to Rotterdam, Bremerhaven, Hamburg and Copenhagen through services provided by Maersk, Baltic Container Line and Team Lines. Other regular services are provided by United Baltic and EuroAfrica to the United Kingdom and Eire, by POL Levant to the Mediterranean, by Chipolbrok to the Far East, plus a variety of regular ferry services across the Baltic from the roll on/roll off ramp in the terminal.

Recent developments have seen the terminal take a part share in Speedcont, providing regular block train connections to the major industrial centres of Poland. Trade on these services has grown dramatically from 5,700 containers in 1995, to some 30,000 in 1997. In addition, there has been recent agreement with the Korean car manufacturer Daewoo, to import car components through the BCT for assembly in Poland, won in keen competition with German ports and Hamburg in particular.

The Baltic General Cargo Terminal (BTDG)

The BTDG became a joint stock company on 1 August 1995. It provides stevedoring, warehousing and handling services for specialised cargo exemplified by exotic fruit and general cargo. Ships with a draft of up to 12.1m can be served. Meanwhile, 165,000 sqm of warehouses and almost the same amount as open storage area are available. There are some 75 cranes of 3 to 16 tonnes capacity, 29 mobile cranes and a workforce of around 1100 people. In 1995 1.7 million tonnes of cargo were handled.

BTDG's activities at the moment are limited by the restricted nature of Gdynia's general cargo traffic and the decline of conventional cargo in particular. A limited amount of paper is handled for export, along with more significant movements of soda and steel products. Bananas are the main cargo - Poland is the world's second biggest consumer of the crop per head after Sweden - and the development of new facilities for exotic fruits centres around this trade.

Future plans are directed towards developing the terminal as a transit facility for traffic to and from the states of the Former Soviet Union and the Baltic States, plus the development of its own Duty Free Zone. The terminal was loss making in 1996 but anticipates a profit in 1997.

The Baltic Grain Terminal (BGT)

This terminal not only handles grain for vessels with a deadweight size of up to 145,000, but it also manages the port's liquid fertiliser facility. Since the port officials see grain handling as the future, a new facility is to be built to increase the present throughput to a desired 3 million tonnes a year.

The terminal is used mainly for the discharge of imported grains and has been completely renovated since 1980. A profitable organisation - with reputed profits of over US$1m in 1996 - cargoes are regularly handled from the Czech Republic and other central European countries and include maize, soya, rape seed, wheat and rye.

The latest improvement has been a new silo raising capacity to over 25,000 tonnes and included redevelopment of the existing pre war silo with new technological facilities.

The Maritime Bulk Terminal (MTMG)

With respect to tonnage, the MTMG has the largest cargo turnover of the port. To become more profitable it is attempting to increase the percentage of high-volume cargo that it processes. Ships with a maximum draft of 10.8 m and a maximum of 30,000 deadweight can be accommodated.

Dry bulk cargoes dominate in Gdynia and they represent the biggest sector in the port with some 3m tonnes in 1995 and 3.5m in 1996. This is dominated by coal exports and limited imports, plus limited quantities of a large number of other commodities including coke breeze, soya, stones and aggregates.

A large number of future developments are planned to compensate for the long decline forecast in the coal industry and these plans are outlined in a later section. MTMG employs around 500 people of whom around 50 are administrative staff.

Other port operating companies

Port Technical Co. Ltd, Port Transport Co. Ltd and Shipping & Port Services Co. Ltd are port operators performing respectively; the maintenance and repair of port and handling equipment, heating engineering, painting and building repairs and security services; port-internal transport services and the maintenance of port transport equipment; and ship-related services including barges, ship repair, tugs, pontoons, floating cranes etc.

The Duty Free Zone of Gdynia

According to Kuzma (1994), a joint stock company "Free Zone Gdynia" had been set up in 1989 with the aim of preparing the legal framework for its operations. Still described as "planned" in the 1996/97 port handbook, the DFZ has now been operating since 25 October 1996 and comprises 33 ha in the eastern and central part of the port. It is managed by the Port Authority which tries to market the zone's benefits to manufacturing, assembling and service companies and which sees prospects for co-operation with Russian and fellow East European enterprises (*Welcome* 1996:16). Its technical and operational characteristics are shown in Table 2.

DFZ Gdynia Technical and Operational Characteristics	
total area	33 ha
storage area (covered)	38,000 sqm
storage area (open)	81,250 sqm
vessels	up to 8.4 m draft
services	technical and communication infrastructure, vessel servicing

Table 2: DFZ Gdynia
Source: Port of Gdynia Handbook 1996/199; *Welcome* (1996:16)

The DFZ enjoys the same tax benefits as the Free Port Zone in Gdańsk or any other national Special Economic Zone as regulated in legislation enacted in 1994. In the Eastern port and next to the ferry terminal, two additional 15 ha sites are reserved for distri-parks. Asian car manufacturers (including

Daewoo of Korea) are said to have shown interest. Part of the Eastern area is being used for storage of imported cars and it is expected that their import will increase further.

Future developments in Gdynia

The Port of Gdynia has considerable plans for the immediate and long term future which they intend to use to build upon the changes in structure, ownership and organisation that have been achieved already. These were detailed in Roe (1998) and are summarised here.

Extensive plans exist for the further development of the Duty Free Zone, both within the central and eastern part of the port. These developments would be a natural progression from the creation of two Special Economic Zones which emerged from the law of 1994 and which have been associated with the Gdynia Shipyard and Dalmor Deepsea Fishing Co. In addition to these developments are two "distri-parks" planned for creation adjacent to the ferry terminal.

Development plans at the Baltic Container Terminal include infra as well as supra structural facilities: e.g. the Helskie I quay extension to 1.2 km, the construction of a new passenger terminal, improved road transport accessibility, the installation of an EDI system and increased TEU handling capacity to 340,000 TEU.

Meanwhile, rather more strategic projects include a new fertiliser export terminal in the eastern part of the port. This terminal will have a capacity of around 300,000 tonnes per annum of both liquid and dry cargo and is a joint development of the port authority and a Polish fertiliser manufacturing company. In addition there are plans for a new oil products terminal, a new cement terminal and packaging plant for the Swedish cement manufacturer Scancem, a series of distri-parks in conjunction with redeveloped ro-ro and container facilities, additional grain storage facilities and the construction of new grain elevators, and a new dedicated alumina terminal. Two new ro-ro berths are planned for rail and road vehicles and two further for road vehicles only.

These latter developments are linked to the construction of new motorways in the region and connections with the planned Trans European Network of highways stretching from Scandinavia in the north to Turkey in the south, and from Germany in the west to Russia in the east. The results of consultants' studies of traffic generation of the port show that some 2.3 million tonnes of cargo will use the Gdynia-Karlskrona ferry route by 2010 including a proportion that is totally new and carried by rail trucks.

Virtually all these proposed developments require some form of external funding outside of the Polish ports industry and the Polish state.

Introduction to the Port of Gdańsk

A brief history

The current situation in the Port of Gdańsk is as much a product of the history of the twentieth century as of any formalised planning process or the effects of the changes that have occurred since 1989 in Poland. Gdańsk - then Danzig - spent much of the first half of the twentieth century outside of any Polish territory that existed at that time. Due to a series of political and historical accidents, despite its long tradition as a port, it was largely neglected from around 1900 to until the 1950s.

In particular, following the end of first world war hostilities, the region around and including Gdańsk was deemed a free city separate from Polish territory and in fact dominated by German controls and interests. This denied Poland a seaport of its own especially since the only alternative was Szczecin and this was part of German territory for much of this time (as Stettin).

As a consequence, the Polish authorities dedicated themselves to the construction of a new port at Gdynia, and Gdańsk was neglected even by the occupying Free City authorities and their allies the Germans. It was only after 1947, and the accession of the new Communist regime that Gdańsk began to be redeveloped and selected as the major bulk terminal for Poland. Liner and subsequently container developments were concentrated at Gdynia. Some spatial specialisation was also apparent with Szczecin (now returned to the Poles) specialising in the Scandinavian markets, and Gdańsk and Gdynia on the Soviet transit and Finnish areas.

Certain current features of the port are a reflection of the traditions and policies of the Communist days - including, for example, the domination of liquid bulk products.

General data

Poland's main bulk port is located at 54°24'N and 18°39'E and actually consists of two ports. The Northern port which is accessible for ships with a draft of 16.5m is located at the mouth of the Vistula river. In 1991 the Northern port was transformed into a limited liability company fully owned by its parent, the Port Authority of Gdańsk. The structure of the authority which is organised by function, is illustrated in Appendix 11. Coal, fuel and crude oil handling dominate in the Northern port. It is here where a container terminal is being built by a North American joint venture. Further details of developments can be found in a later section.

The Inner port handles grain, timber, phosphate, general cargo and sulphur. It is the berthing place for ferries to and from Scandinavia. A look at the port handling statistics in Appendix 12 reveals that coal and liquid fuel are the biggest commodity group handled.

Although the port appreciates its promising position (*Lloyd's List* 1995, May) as the major liquid bulk port in Poland, it nevertheless continues to attempt to diversify into containers (traditionally Gdynia's business), grain transhipment and cruise ship servicing (Zarzad Portu Gdańsk 1996).

The amount of total cargo handled has dropped by 3.7% from 22.9 mt in 1993 to an estimated 22.7 mt in 1995. Whereas liquid bulk handling fell by 15%, containers showed an increase of over 700%. However, 1993 showed only a very low figure of 700 t (*Lloyd's List* 1995, May).

The port authority undertakes purely management related tasks (as the landlord authority) since it started to privatise the port as early as 1990. The topic of privatisation is the subject of a later section.

Port turnover

Bulk commodities dominate in the port of Gdańsk as we have already seen and these in turn are characterised by a limited number of specialisms derived largely from the Communist dominated days prior to 1989.

Coal

Coal is easily the most significant commodity that moves through the port, representing some 39% of throughput in 1995 at 7.1m tonnes. However, coal has been on continuous decline since 1993 and recent figures (e.g. the fall from 4.13m tonnes in the first half of 1995 to 2.81m tonnes) are both significant and substantial in their reduction.

The coal terminal is located in the Northern Port and has the benefits of full automation and the ability to process 50,000 tonnes a day and to store 600,000 tonnes. The changing world energy market, however, is resulting in a sizeable underuse of this facility.

Liquid fuels

Liquid fuels form the second biggest traffic flow through Gdańsk with some 35.2% of cargo in 1995. Gdańsk has an almost complete monopoly on the import of liquid fuels into Poland unlike the coal trade where Szczecin retains a major proportion of the market. Its characteristics as a market are also rather more buoyant than that of the coal trades as the Polish economy continues to make its moves away from the heavy industry dominated characteristics of the past (demanding large coal supplies) to that of an oil based society with no domestic sources. Around 6.4 million tonnes were processed in 1995.

The processing facilities in Gdańsk have been connected to refineries in Germany for many years and also have direct links by pipeline into and out of the Former Soviet Union. At times, these links, even in recent years, have been useful but in general terms the Polish refiners are attempting to make Poland a more independent location for oil refining and acquisition, and not reliant upon imports from Russia. The establishment of Naftoport is a collaboration between the state companies of Gdańsk Refinery, Plock Petrochemia, Pern pipeline, Polska Żegluga Morska (PZM) and the Central Oil Product Agency. This development increased oil handling capabilities from 6 million tonnes to 12-13 million tonnes a year, thus facilitating the fulfilment of domestic needs.

The new facility has been a US$26m investment with two new berths for tankers up to 150,000 dwt - the largest that can enter and leave the Baltic Sea. In addition, a 25 year lease for a new gas terminal was agreed in 1994 following the signing of a US$30 million contract with gas importer and distributor Gaspol (owned by a combination of Polish gas distributors and a Dutch joint venture). The terminal will have an annual capacity of around 500,000 cu. m. and cost US$22 million for the first phase opened in April 1997 including new gas tank facilities and a new berth.

Other bulk

Other bulk is the third largest category of traffic and represents around 15% of cargo and around 3 million tonnes.

General cargo

General cargo represents the next largest category despite the weak general cargo base that the port retains. Some 1.7 million tonnes were processed in 1995 representing around 10% of the turnover of the port. The trend however is a decline in traffic which the port is attempting to meet through investments such as the Duty Free Zone. Regular liner services are offered to only a few destinations including Turkish Cargo lines to Izmir, Mersin, Istanbul and Derince; PNSC to Karachi in Pakistan and Dammam in Saudi

Arabia; ENC to Alexandria in Egypt, and SC India to Bombay, Calcutta and Madras.

Other categories

Other categories of cargo include liquid sulphur, phosphorites, grain, soda, timber, pulp and construction timber which together represented some 10% of the total traffic of the port.

The Wolny Obszar Celny (Port Free Zone)

The WOC was established by Order of the Minister Council on 28 November 1995 (Legislation No. 141, Art 693) and has been operating since October 15 of the following year. It occupies a 33.5 ha area situated around the Władyslawa IV basin at the port entrance of the Northern port. Further technical characteristics can be taken from Table 3.

Ownership and administration are vested entirely in the Port Authority of Gdańsk; it also issues the required operating licences to foreign and national commercial enterprises. From a legal point of view, the WOC is Polish national but tax-free territory. This brings the benefit of a cargo movement into the WOC from abroad and vice-versa unimpaired by contingent restrictions or tax and duties; likewise, goods manufactured or assembled in the port free zone enjoy preferential tax treatment when imported into Poland.

Under the new Polish legislation, the following activities may be carried out in the WOC by Polish, overseas and/or international companies:

> cargo handling
> cargo storage
> manufacturing
> product assembly
> forwarding and transport
> insurance
> consultancy

The advantages the WOC presents over and above the conventional port consist of the following:

> Payment of customs duties and VAT deferred until the goods enter Polish customs territory.
> Waived customs guarantee payments.

Reduced customs duties and VAT liabilities on goods processed in the WOC.
Increased security (CCTV, guards, fence and floodlighting).

WOC Gdańsk Technical and Operational Characteristics	
total area	33,5 ha
storage area (covered)	49,000 sqm
storage area (open)	80,000 sqm
operating quays	6
	total length: 850 m
vessels	up to 174 m length
	up to 8.4 m draft
services	vessel servicing and cargo handling facilities

Table 3: WOC Gdańsk
Source: Zarzad Portu Gdańsk (1997a, b)

In its marketing publications the Port Authority encourages investment in the free zone by production and manufacturing companies, international distribution and logistics firms including freight forwarders and trading companies which target the markets of central Europe and the Former Soviet Union.

The WOC took some time to establish itself and it wasn't until 1997 that there was any real evidence of economic activity. One associated development has been the establishment of a shipping link to Kaliningrad in Russia and the opening of a regional office there. This development was part of the process of attempting to attract transit traffic to the port from the Former Soviet Union. One problem in attempting to acquire much of this traffic is the lack of a traditional container port base at Gdańsk even though the technical facilities do exist. Logistical facilities also need to be improved. By summer 1997 some 35 customers had been attracted to the WOC with particular specialisms focusing upon steel and timber traffic.

Other port development activities

Ore and grain terminals

A new iron ore terminal is planned by the Polish owned steel mills Huta Katowice in collaboration with a Brazilian iron ore exporters. Completion is due in 1998 and capacity will be around 3-5 million tonnes a year from the 30 ha. site. The existing ore quay in the Northern port is currently used for steel products and will not be converted for ore use. It is hoped that both Czech Republic and Slovakian importers will be attracted to the new facility. Total investment is around US$50m.

There has also been an agreement reached with Europort of the USA/Canada to develop a new grain import terminal with a capacity of between 2 and 4 million tonnes a year located on the old Soviet ore pier facility. The aim is to attract the larger vessels that normally trade through Hamburg and the terminal will also include facilities for the processing of feedstuffs. In total it will cover around 56ha of the port area. The major target markets are the countries of the Former Soviet Union and the new facility will provide storage for around 150,000 tonnes of grain at a berth with a depth of 16.5m and a usable length of 300m. A further stage would include additional cranes and storage facilities. Total cost is estimated at US$145m. Investors in the consortium include Saskatchewan Wheat Pool which would manage the facility, Dessaport International, a Halifax (Canada) based engineering company, and a USA based development company. Construction was due to start in December 1997 with completion expected in late 1999.

Liquid fuels and coal terminal development

The development of a new LPG terminal began in 1995 and was completed in Spring 1997. Here, the main objective was the facilitation of the import of petrol from Norway in minimum amounts of 800,000 tonnes a year. The project was financed by the jointly owned UK, Dutch, and Polish company Gaspol which possesses a 75% market share of Polish petroleum products in a very fast growing market. Meanwhile, the construction of a third oil pier in the port will, with the other developments in this sector, bring the capacity of Gdańsk up to 35m tonnes p.a. of liquid fuels. Much of this growth is based upon the inherited and extensive pipeline network put in place by the old regimes in Poland, the Soviet Union and the DDR. Gdańsk is able to supply directly, the German refineries of Schwedt and Leuna at highly competitive rates. 17m tonnes of this liquid fuel capacity is for oil handling, providing plenty of room at present for Polish needs and transit traffic. Some 4m tonnes moves annually to Germany through an agreement with Naftoport. Total investment should be around US$23m.

Highway development

One of the major infrastuctural developments in Poland occurring at the moment and as a direct response to the economic changes that have taken place in the 1990s, is the planned improvement of the highway network. Under the old regime, highways were considered very secondary in status and importance after the rail network for inland distribution and received little funding reflected still today in their low quality and inadequate capacity for modern logistical needs. The port access roads were no exception to this general rule, and in the north of the country, following the social, political and economic changes of the late 1980s, there were no motorways and few dual carriageway facilities. Road surfaces were inadequate, road signing poor, drainage of low quality and other facilities (e.g. services, lighting and safety provision) were substandard. Through the 1990s, plans were developed for the improvement of road facilities and in the Gdańsk (and Gdynia) area the new A1 motorway has been proposed and designed to improve access to the ports and to link the Tricity of Gdańsk, Gdynia and Sopot, with Warsaw and beyond. Unfortunately, although the physical planning is complete, there remain difficulties in attracting private investment through the assembly of a consortium and agreement of the precise financial arrangements, necessary as the Polish state cannot afford to build these new roads without it, and international governmental investors (e.g. the European Union) are unprepared to finance them alone. Once the financial arrangements can be at least partially agreed, there will be a public tendering process to select the preferred consortium bidder. Additional highway improvements will include new links to the Gdańsk by pass and the nearby airport at Rębiechowo to be financed by the World Bank.

In addition to this major motorway development, which incidentally will form part of the Trans European Motorway between Scandinavia and south-east Europe and Turkey, utilising the ferry links that currently serve Gdańsk and Gdynia, funding has been agreed again with the World Bank and the Polish Ministry of Transport in October 1996, for the construction of a new 1400m road bridge over the River Wistula to the east of the city eventually linking in with the new motorway system and a variety of connecting highways that will improve access to the port and relieve local congestion. A whole new area of the port, to the south east of other developments, will then be opened up for container and ro-ro traffic which is currently almost non-existent in Gdańsk. The new bridge will be finished by 1999 at a cost of US$26m. This fits in nicely with the anticipated container capacity problems for Gdynia from around 2002. The Baltic Container Terminal in Gdynia has no room for expansion because it is surrounded by the city itself and with the growth of the Polish and Former Soviet Union economies it is anticipated that container traffic, in particular, will expand substantially.

Other developments

A variety of other developments in the port are either underway or proposed. These include a cement and asphalt plant in connection with the expansion of the Polish road building programme; a new malt factory, funded to the tune of 14m DEM and owned by German interests plus the International Finance Corporation which should be completed during 1998 and will provide 50% of output for Polish consumption and 50% for export - annual capacity will be 120,000 tonnes of malt from 170,000 tonnes of barley; new pier facilities funded by the Port Authority, for which, as yet (1997), there are no designated purposes but which openly display confidence in the port; further liquid chemical developments which although expected to cause some environmental problems and meet environmental resistance, are likely to be attracted to Gdańsk where sites are available, unlike Gdynia where the proximity of the city makes such developments impossible; and roll on-roll off ferry developments which, at present remain very insecure. Recent (1996) loss of the Helsinki service because of a failure to use an appropriate ship orientated towards a freight market and thus disappointing loadings, has left Gdańsk with only the (PZB) Oxelsund/Nynashamn route which runs three times weekly in the winter and daily in the summer. However, the Gdańsk ferry terminal operated by a separate semi-private company - Sirkopol (in effect PZB, the state ferry company) - is both old and small and in need of urgent replacement in particular to facilitate the use of modern, larger ferries. Plans exist for its redevelopment at the Obroncow Westerplatte Quay, costing US$2m and includes new parking facilities for trucks and some additional highway improvements.

The Polish environment[2]

The Polish economic, political and social transformation resulted first of all in substantial internal turbulence. Although inflation has decreased from the dizzy heights of 900% in 1989/90, it remains in mid 1998 rather high with an annual level of around 19% in 1997. In 1996 the złoty lost 14% against the US$, although the figure for the first half of 1997 was slightly lower at

---

[2] This subchapter uses information from Szwankowski (1994, 1996), Tubielewicz (1994, 1995), Kuzma (1994a, b), Dobrowolski (1994a, b), Misztal (1994a, b, 1996).

11.8% (Euromoney 1997:3). After its 1995 high of 7%, the GDP has been falling since - albeit slowly - and stands at 6% for the first half of 1997 (Polish Embassy 1997).

As other East European countries followed the Polish approach to transformation and thus suffered similar economic problems, Polish ports were hit by the geographical shift in trade flows - a consequence of transport as a derived demand and its ultimate impact upon the international ports and transport industries. Whereas in 1990 around 40% of exports and imports were undertaken in trade with the highly competitive European Union (EU) markets and 23% with the former COMECON countries, the share of EU trade had risen to an average of 67% in 1995 whilst trade with former COMECON countries had declined to a mere 16% (Polish Embassy 1997). At present, Germany is Poland's biggest trade partner with around 30% of both exports and imports.

In the development of their model and later survey regarding the influences of environmental change upon the Polish shipping industry, Ledger and Roe (1993:240,1996) identified several particularly significant issues that dominate: the development of democratic institutions, the influence of state withdrawal/privatisation from the appropriate commercial or industrial sector, the emergence of joint ventures and co-operation with the west, the continuing problems and role of hard currency and the residual (and substantial) infrastructural problems. As regards Polish ports it is clear that particularly the issues relating to state withdrawal/privatisation, the creation of a free market economy and hard currency issues stand out. In addition, since transport is a derived demand, the economic and political changes in other countries are highly influential upon Polish port throughput.

Free market economy and competition

It is claimed by the Polish port authorities that the free market economy in Polish terms means for the ports, that unlike in the large majority of other European countries, subsidies to the industry and its main domestic market players have been completely withdrawn. In addition, any form of co-ordinating hand from the Ministry of Transport and Maritime Trade, that used to be so important, is missing. Severely affected by the major political and economic changes in other (East) European countries, Polish ports now face competition that Kuzma (1996, 1997) identified was fourfold in nature and impact:

competition with other European ports
competition with other Polish ports
competition with other modes of transport
competition within each port itself.

To begin with the latter, cutting prices as a means of competition between the undercapitalised operators in the port of Gdańsk has now reached the point that several operators are unable to perform adequate services due to a lack of capital. This will have clear ramifications in the medium to long term for the prosperity of the port community as a whole.

Interport competition between Gdynia and Gdańsk has a strong historical background and dates from the earliest days of the development of Gdynia in the 1920s. As long as there are no co-ordinating efforts undertaken by the government, Gdańsk will continue to try to enter the grain and container market and Gdynia, in a similar fashion, will try to enter the liquid bulk handling market.

As regards competition with foreign ports and other modal transport operators, it can be best understood after an examination of the ports' hinterland and the transport corridors through Poland and Eastern Europe. It is generally agreed, and reflected in current EU policy towards the development of Trans European Networks, that two North-South corridors from Scandinavia to Southern Europe pass through Poland: one passes through Szczecin-Świnoujście region in the west of Poland whilst the second follows the designated A1 motorway through the Gdynia-Gdańsk port complex. There also exists a clear transport corridor in an East-West direction through the northern region of Poland linking the Szczecin/Świnoujście complex with Gdańsk and Gdynia, the Baltic States and the Kaliningrad enclave with reasonable rail links (and incidentally poor road links) into the Former Soviet Union.

Under the old regime, Gdynia and Gdańsk's hinterland comprised the domestic territory of Poland and its communist neighbours, including the former Czechoslovakia, Hungary and the Former Soviet Union. Today, the hinterland has changed considerably with a reduced area of a radius of 100-200 km around the ports (Kuzma 1997). The remainder is now open to competitors from the road and rail industry collaborating with Gdynia's and Gdańsk's major competitors: Hamburg, Rotterdam, the eastern German ports in particular Rostock as well as other Baltic ports. An example of the competitive framework is the degree to which Polzug's transportation system (the private rail/intermodal operator) has already penetrated the traditional hinterland including block train services from the Katowice, Łódź and Warsaw areas to north German ports and beyond.

The World Bank's *Port Sector Study Poland* (1994) revealed that regarding container handling and hinterland transit, transportation through Polish ports at present tends to be uncompetitive in terms of price. It is however, competitive with respect to bulk and conventional general cargo. Help from the European Union to redress this situation cannot be expected as the PACT programme seems to favour land transport routes when promoting combined transport (see Baker 1997).

Privatisation

Bałcerowicz's economic restructuring plan of 1990 for Poland, foresaw two methods of privatisation: that of capital privatisation and direct privatisation[3] (Dobrowolski 1994b, Misztal 1993). The former involves the transformation of large/medium-size enterprises into state treasury companies before their shares are sold; the latter is applied to medium/small firms which are sold after liquidation to private entrepreneurs. After 1992 further privatisation methods were introduced. The National Investment Fund Programme (NIFP) allows each National Investment Fund (NIF) to be listed on the Warsaw Stock Exchange. Under privatisation through restructuring, a management group will be allowed to buy up to 80% of the shares of the company after it has carried out successfully, an approved restructuring programme in that particular company. The Stabilisation, Restructuring and Privatisation Programme (SRP) allows privatisation of companies which are deemed to be in extremely poor financial and commercial shape (Embassy of the Republic of Poland 1997).

The Port Act of 1996

For Polish ports the method of capital privatisation had been chosen by the state Ministry (Dobrowolski and Szwankowski 1997) and the relevant legal regulation is the 1996 Port Act which will came into effect in late 1997 and which in mid 1998 was only just having some tangible effect. It provides the long awaited legal basis for the privatisation activities which started as early as 1990.

At present the ownership structure of the ports' *areas* is as shown in Figure 11.

---

[3] as laid down in the Act on Privatisation of State-owned Enterprises of 13 July 1990 and which was replaced by the Act on Commercialisation and Privatisation of State-owned Enterprises of 30 August 1996.

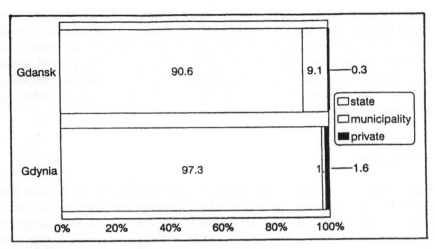

Figure 11: Ownership of port areas in 1996-97
Source: Dobrowolski and Szwankowski (1997)

As regards the ownership of the *port enterprise*, that is the port authorities and Gdynia's terminals, the state is owner of 100% of these activities and the associated infrastructure. At the same time, it is widely maintained that both the ports of Gdańsk and Gdynia are now fully privatised. Taking into consideration that privatisation is "simply the transfer of ownership ... from the public to the private sector" (Thomas 1994), it is more appropriate to look at this transformation process as a restructuring process (Dobrowolski and Szwankowski 1997) where the legal make-up and the structure have been changed. The desired outcome of this process will eventually be full privatisation of the operating companies and a mixed state-municipality-private ownership of the port authorities.

Figure 12a shows the pre-privatisation structure of the merchant seaport enterprise in Poland and applicable to both Gdynia and Gdańsk: a "one port - one enterprise" model (Tubielewicz 1995:20). A monolith, fully state-owned, it performed all functions of the port including administration and operational functions as well as a large number of non-port related activities. Its maintenance and development plans were valid only in the port area it controlled whilst co-ordinated development activities with other enterprises operating in the port did not exist.

Under the 1996 Port Act the port authority will perform all administrative functions and will be responsible for the maintenance and the development of the infrastructure for the *whole* port (see Figure 12b). The state will hold 51% of the shares, and both municipalities of Gdynia and Gdańsk 34%; the remainder may be held by private owners. The economic functions, on the other hand, will be carried out by fully independent operators. Initially they may still be subsidiaries of the port authority like in Gdynia. The final goal is to achieve full privatisation including large scale investment from outside the port industry.

Privatisation in the Ports of Gdynia and Gdańsk

In the absence of specific legal stipulations, the two ports had been free to go their own way in privatising the port enterprises. But, more importantly, this lack of a legal framework has resulted in a privatisation process that was not accompanied by an appropriate reform of the port area management (Dobrowolski and Szwankowski 1997).

Under the old system, there was no single entity which co-ordinated the overall development of the port (Tubielewicz 1995:20). As shown in Figure 12a, there were several bodies operating in the port boundaries, one of them being the merchant seaport. With the 1996 Port Act a new port authority is to be created. Its tasks, as outlined above in an earlier section and shown in Figure 12b, comprise the maintenance and development of the whole port, thus making general development plans for all enterprises in the port, be they operators, free port zones, industries or otherwise.

PORT AUTHORITY : OWNERSHIP AND STRUCTURE PRIOR TO PRIVATISATION

One port - one enterprise model. 100% state owned

Port Authority. Merchant sea port

Administration	Economic/Operational function	Others
Maintenance and development of port infrastructure	Terminals	Welfare
	Warehouses	Holiday resorts
	Tugs	Retailing
	Intraport transport	

Figure 12a: Port ownership and structure prior to privatisation and in compliance with the 1996 Port Act
Source: Authors

Privatisation in the Port of Gdynia[4]

Subsequent to a ministerial decision in 1991, the port enterprise was transformed into "Morski Port Handlowy Gdynia S.A." (Merchant Sea Port Gdynia S.A.). In order to prepare a successful transformation, port officials set up a series of teams to integrate employers and ensure full co-operation. In 1994 and 1995 seven fully capitalised companies were separated from the Merchant Sea Port Holding and equipped with the capital of the holding. In the near future, and hopefully during 1998, following the stipulations of the 1996 Port Act, the present port authority will be transformed into a public (non-profit making) enterprise. At the same time shares in the four terminals and three support service companies will be issued and sold to either the general public or to other organisations. As yet no specific date has been set for this transformation.

PORT OWNERSHIP AND STRUCTURE IN COMPLIANCE WITH THE 1996 PORT ACT

Ownership Port Authority: Others - 25%/15%
State - 51%
Municipality - 24/34%

Ownership private or
port subsidiary   Private - 100%

Port Authority

Administration and maintenance

Subsidiaries

Private or port operating subsidiaries

Operator 1   Operator 2   Operator 3   Operator n...

Figure 12b: Port ownership and structure in compliance with the 1996 Port Act
Source: Authors

---

[4] This subchapter follows Kuzma (1996 and 1994).

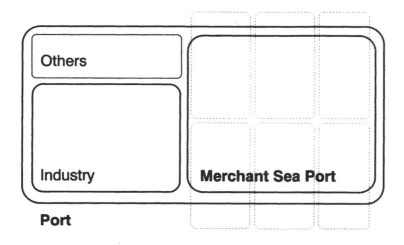

Figure 13 : Systems diagram: Polish ports before privatisation
Source: Authors

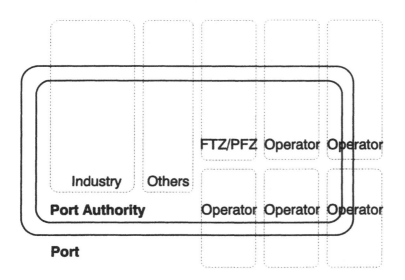

Figure 14: Systems diagram: Polish ports in compliance with the 1996 Port Act
Source: Authors

Privatisation in the Port of Gdańsk

In contrast to Gdynia's incremental approach towards privatisation, the port of Gdańsk has taken a direct road. Following its transformation into "Morski Port Handlowy Gdańsk S.A." in 1991, the first and immediate action was to divest a series of non-port related businesses including hospitals, schools and holiday resorts with the specific aim of restoring liquidity. In a second step, 30 limited liability companies were separated off, with the Morski Port holding 55% of the shares. On 22 September 1993 the remaining body of the Morski Port enterprise was transformed into today's "Zarzad Portu Gdańsk" whilst at the same time its shares in each of the operating companies were sold. With the new port authority taking responsibility for maintenance and development of the port infrastructure, Gdańsk became the first port of Poland to obtain a true separation of the operational and infrastructural sphere.

Hard currency issues

The Polish port officials state that they need and want to modernise their ports in order to stay or become competitive. To have any hope of this, substantial sums of foreign investment are needed. (Gdańsk talks of a "Billion dollar port" (Gdańsk Port Handbook 1996)). However, whether investors can be found depends not only upon the future prospects of the ports but also upon the general economic situation and upon exchange rate stability. Poland's "Package 2000", the 1996 programme of fiscal and macroeconomic policies, projects an average annual GDP increase of around 5.4%. It also targets an inflation rate of 4.9% in the year 2000 (Embassy of the Republic of Poland 1997) - which is 14.1% points down from the present figure in 1997.[5] Such achievement certainly would increase the chances of Polish ports to attract foreign capital but may be rather unrealistic given the position only three years before its objective date.

Some concluding issues

This section is largely derived from earlier work by Roe (1998) which examined the role of privatisation in the state organisations of the Polish maritime sector. We shall examine conclusions for each of the two ports in turn.

---

[5] telephone enquiry, Embassy of Poland, Information Department, September 1997.

58

There is considerable developmental activity in the Port of Gdańsk, which reflects the sizeable political, economic and social changes that have occurred in Poland and more specifically, the impact of commercialisation and potential privatisation in the ports sector. The creation of a series of new stevedoring companies in a form suitable for privatisation at short notice reflects the attitude of the port towards the future and is mirrored, to a certain extent, by the number and range of new port projects that are either proposed or actually in a state of development. It is inevitable that some of these proposals will never see the light of day as the funding that they need may not be available and the markets to which they are directed may never emerge. However, the sheer volume and number of projects implies a faith in the future of the port and a recognition that change must and will occur. No longer can Gdańsk survive upon the limited markets it was once allocated by the state and there is a pressing need to improve the physical facilities utilised by the existing market sectors and to begin to direct energies towards the revitalisation of new ones.

The new ownership structure of the port, resulting from the Ports Act which came into force during 1997, will push the Port Authority further down the line towards privatisation, matching the moves of the operating and stevedoring companies. Gdańsk will at least possess the basis for this privatisation and has recognised the new spatial markets that it needs to enter including those with enormous potential in the Former Soviet Union and the Kaliningrad enclave, the Baltic States, the Ukraine and Belarus in particular. Polish domestic sources of trade - either import or export - cannot support the level of activity in any of the existing Polish international ports (Gdańsk, Gdynia or Szczecin/Świnoujście) that would be needed to provide a profitable base, and thus to survive the rigours of privatisation, new markets must be found. However, some doubt has to be expressed about the likely possibilities of Gdańsk achieving a viable level of trade particularly in the general cargo markets where Gdynia's pre-eminence in the container trades makes progress elsewhere somewhat difficult. This is even with the anticipated and widely acknowledged growth in container trades that is bound to occur with the gradual, and inevitable, growth of the economies of central and eastern Europe. Similar comments can be made about the roll on/roll off ferry market, where considerable growth again can be anticipated with the developments in Central and Eastern Europe, the integration of Sweden and Finland into the European Union and the eventual construction and opening of the Trans European Motorway network in southern and eastern regions of the continent. Gdynia's advantage that it holds with current facilities, and its locational advantage nearer the open Baltic Sea unconstrained to a narrow site with outdated facilities, may mean that developments in Gdańsk are very difficult to encourage. The loss of the growing Helsinki market is indicative of the problems that are faced.

Some comments can also be made about the relationship that exists between the new stevedoring companies and the Port Authority. In theory there is no conflict. The new companies are independent of the authority and must make profits to survive at least in the long term, adapting to market conditions and opportunities as they see fit. In practice, there is undoubtedly some form of cross-subsidy going on to ensure that those stevedoring operations which have inherited the less prosperous areas of activity - for example general cargo - remain supported by the more active ones (for example the coal and oil terminal workers). Despite Port Authority claims that each stevedoring company retains its own profits and faces the risk of going bankrupt, there seems to be an active process of support to ensure that this does not take place which cannot continue with full privatisation. In addition, the Port Authority claims to negotiate appropriate leasing charges for services and equipment which ensure that the stevedoring companies do not go bankrupt - in other words they are treated favourably - because they constitute old employees of the port. As new (private) companies emerge who wish to lease equipment (for example), they are treated more "economically realistically". Some doubt has to be raised about the merits of this sort of approach within a free market situation in the ports industry of Poland as a whole where the competitive environment is becoming increasingly apparent and unavoidable. In addition to these problems, the port has also expressed concern over its inability to attract credit from both domestic and international institutions because of its new structure and the large number of small operating units that now exist. This may present problems in the future for the other Polish ports as well.

Finally, in terms of Gdańsk, two issues; firstly, considerable hopes are pinned upon the new Duty Free Zone. However, Gdańsk, as with all Polish ports, is a very late entry into this market in the Baltic region as a whole and may find it difficult to prove attractive over and above established competitors and those new competitors emerging all the time in locations such as St Petersburg, the Baltic States, the new revitalised eastern länder of Germany and even Poland itself (e.g. Gdynia). Secondly, the political significance of Gdańsk as a port location should not be overlooked and the 1997 troubles relating to the bankrupt shipyard are indicative of this.

A number of interesting issues also emerge from the outline of the Port of Gdynia and its activities in recent years.

In terms of the port's organisation and organisational structure, quite considerable changes can be seen to have occurred stimulated by a combination of state force and a recognition of need. Thus the new operating companies represent a major move from the old system of management and provide extensive opportunities for future privatisation and development of new markets and services. The latter is beginning to occur although, quite understandably, only slowly. Privatisation will follow of the operating companies although the exact form is unknown - and there is no doubt that these privatised units have a good opportunity to prosper in the new economic climate. In contrast, the old port authority will remain in public hands - albeit somewhat different ones with the introduction of local city interests which at least should help to stimulate the organisation into being more locally responsive. This may restrict developments and hinder ideas that are potentially of benefit to the port and its users. The strategic argument that ports need to be in state hands remains predominant in Poland unlike elsewhere (e.g. UK) where port privatisation of management and ownership (including land) is increasingly common. Possibly time will tell, and with the potential success of the privatised operators, the authority could follow.

One major change in the port has been the growth in number of overseas users since the economic and political changes of the late 1980s exemplified by Copenhagen based Maersk (container) Line and its weekly service to Denmark, the Netherlands, and Germany feeding into its international container line network and that of German shipping company Team Lines with a similar service to Bremerhaven and Hamburg. This trend will continue and will help to force the port authority to consider its future strategy with respect to markets and reorganisation.

The port is generally profitable (e.g. around old Zł600bn in 1993 and old Zł168bn in 1994), with the variation largely explicable by variations in coal and to a lesser extent, grain throughput. This does not, of course, take account of the indirect subsidies available from the state in the form of major infrastructural grants, and also those from overseas international bodies (e.g. the World Bank).

Overall, there is considerable activity in the ports sector typified by the action in the Port of Gdynia. However, Gdynia presents a rather less political profile than that of its neighbour Gdańsk with its shipyard problems. Much more action is soon to follow with further commercialisation steps and the inevitable march towards privatisation. In many ways this matches the steps already taken in the shipping sector with, for example, the creation of subsidiary companies in PZM and Polish Ocean Lines which are distanced from the parent but ready for further moves towards the private sector. This last stage is a difficult one to accomplish but is increasingly becoming a fact of life following the restructuring of port activities and ownership.

Conclusions

As a result of the transformation process in Poland and its neighbouring countries, Polish ports find themselves operating in a fourfold competitive environment. In addition their traditional hinterland is being eroded by other transport mode providers and foreign ports. Nevertheless, the prognosis for the development of turnover in the ports of Gdynia and Gdańsk in 2010 (Appendix 12) is very positive. Gdynia and Gdańsk will be major players in the transit of goods to and from the Former Soviet Union. It is a required move however, that the ports restructure themselves as distribution centres and actively seek an integration into the East and West European transport chain and network.

4. Conceptual models and methodology

Introduction

The conceptual models which form the basis to this research need now to be introduced, before the methodological issues and results of this study of port transformation in Poland are presented in later chapters.

Conceptual model of the strategic planning process

The conceptual model of the strategic planning process has already been introduced and discussed in Chapter Two when the strategic planning process was analysed in some depth. We shall not dwell on this model further here but note the earlier discussion simply from the point of view of completeness.

Conceptual model of the strategic management system in relation to the (perceived) turbulence level of the environment

One aim of this study is to analyse whether

> a) the strategic management systems of the ports of Gdynia and Gdańsk relate to the degree of (perceived) environmental turbulence; and whether

b) inter-port variations can be observed although both ports have been and are subject to almost identical environmental influences.

Figure 15 provides a graphical summary of the conceptual model.

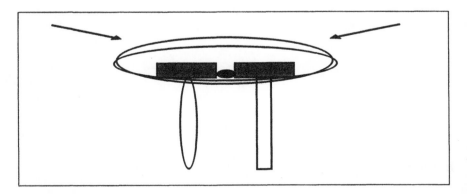

Figure 15: Conceptual model of the strategic management systems of the Ports of Gdynia and Gdańsk in relation to the turbulence level of the environment
Source: Authors

In this model the rectangles represent the two ports. The circle in between is to symbolise that both ports share almost the same location. Environmental forces represented by arrows shape and deform the environment as indicated by the ellipses. The strategic management systems upon which the strategic decision-making in the ports is built may exhibit particular features. This is illustrated by the oval and rectangular shape of the "strategy pillars".

This graphical illustration of the environment in which strategy is developed within the Polish ports industry provides the framework for the following discussion and the survey of opinion and attitude of the port authorities and operating companies.

Methodology

Following the brief outline of the conceptual models, this chapter continues to provide detailed information and analysis regarding the methodology of the study. It addresses the issue of sampling and explains and justifies the characteristics of the data collection methods that were chosen to ensure validity, generalisability and objectivity of the study. The chapter closes by showing how a series of design issues were tackled in order to maximise data quality output and thus improve and sustain the quality and reliability of the results.

Sample

The focus of this study is upon the internal process of strategy development in port authorities and as a consequence, port authority and port operating company officials were identified as the target respondents. Information regarding external data was obtained by conducting relatively unstructured interviews with government and municipality officials as well as members of relevant academic institutions and research institutes within the region. Further data was gathered from books, periodicals, newspapers and journals of the university maritime libraries in Plymouth and Cardiff in the United Kingdom, and Sopot, Poland as well as from port publications, unpublished internal documents and government publications.

Polish statistics were available in a format that was very current but had the disadvantage of being only in Polish. This did not prevent their usage but did inhibit their interpretation to a certain extent Only occasionally did they have an English summary. Regarding a substantial number of legal issues such as the 1996 Port Act and the future competencies of the Urzad Morski (Polish State Maritime Office), this contrasted with the large majority of the data made available by the newly created Gdynia Port Authority, as it was available only in Polish and therefore its interpretation was limited and its application thus constrained.

The five port authority board members each of the boards of Gdynia and Gdańsk, the four directors of the Gdynia terminals and the commercial senior executive of the Gdańsk WOC were all contacted to obtain advice, opinion and information. The Gdynia terminal directors were included in the list of respondents since, as was illustrated in Chapter Three, these terminals are (still) subsidiaries of the port authority. Three officials were interviewed in person and in full structured format. To enlarge the sample size and thus improve the reliability and validity of the results, questionnaires were also mailed with a covering letter to the remaining officials. Follow-up (telephone) interviews were then conducted at a later date.

There was considerable difficulty in obtaining primary information from both ports and in some circumstances, the main sources of data were published materials from a large number of origins including the publicity material of the ports and other published commentaries from elsewhere. The reluctance to speak out can be attributed at least in part to the main topic of the research - i.e. the concept of strategic management in ports in Poland - where the new economic, political and legal environment coupled with the legacies of the past have left many senior managers with a fear of being open about their approaches, a feeling of inadequacy compared with port managers in the west and a overhang from the old regimes where such details were never made public.

However, it was possible for the research to analyse the material from elsewhere along with the primary data that was made available and the opinions expressed by a limited number of port managers.

Methods of data collection

Out of the wide spectrum of research methods applied in strategic management, it was decided within this study to employ a field based research approach, a method eminently capable of analysing real-life organisations in their natural environment as opposed to computer or other forms of simulation that deal with controlled experiments lying at the other end of the experimental spectrum (Snow and Thomas 1994).

To collect the different types of data that were needed, various methods were theoretically available. For soft data (the organisational climate, external and internal culture, organisational resistance to change) as well as for the verification of hard data obtained from the questionnaires (for example concerning the generation of strategies and the strategic process) direct observation would have been the most desirable approach. However, observation of this type requires a lengthy amount of time and extensive resources (Mintzberg as referenced in Snow and Thomas 1994:459) and therefore had to be dismissed in the context of this work.

In order to keep a maximum of flexibility and adaptability, and to allow an exploration of relevant issues on the one side, but to be able to guarantee on the other side that the same issues would be discussed with the same respondent, a semi-structured interview appeared most appropriate. Another major argument in favour of a direct interviewed approach was that the topic of research consisted of so many varied aspects that the choice and "codification" of a fixed set of questions into a formal questionnaire would inevitably have missed out important issues. Prior to the site visit the key topics that needed to be addressed were identified and for each topic highly structured sequences of questions and prompts were prepared.

Following the first interviews it was clear that a problem was arising that respondents tended to answer questions but only in terms of strategic content. This lead to a radical change in the research method and to overcome this problem, a questionnaire with closed questions was designed. Using the knowledge gained from the interviews, the original list of topics was narrowed down to those which had emerged as the most highly relevant. Meanwhile, the length was kept at the upper limit of what was felt to be reasonable for respondents, and yet still ensured that all the necessary information was obtained.

Another point was taken into consideration which justified the modification of the research method. Several officials had indicated that they would not be able to keep the appointments made. Therefore the questionnaire was also designed with the view that it could be sent by mail as self-completed questionnaires. The design implications which arose are discussed in a later section.

Conduct of interviews and questionnaire design

General issues

To have any true value, scientific enquiry needs to be trustworthy and the traditional issues which have been widely identified in this respect surround the issues of validity, objectivity and generalisability (Robson 1993).

Validity can be impaired by many inadequacies but perhaps by subject/observer errors and bias in particular. The measures taken to minimise the occurrence of these problems are described later in the sections which detail the conduct of interviews which were carried out and the questionnaire design.

A study must also be able to show causal relationship (i.e. have internal validity). In this context, one major objective of this study was to analyse whether there exists a link between the level of turbulence in the ports' operating environment and that which exists in the ports' strategic management system.

The choice of Gdańsk and Gdynia ports in this context centred around two main issues:

> (1) Firstly, research (UNCTAD 1993:8) results suggest that the port size correlates directly and closely with the formality of the port planning process and the response type. The bigger that the port is, the more explicit and pro-active planning that is undertaken tends to be - and the easier it will be to recognise and analyse a process of strategic management. Poland's most significant and largest ports are Gdańsk, Gdynia and Szczecin-Świnoujście. The first two are those

central to this study and by the nature of their size and importance, the process of strategic management recognition should be that much easier to identify.

(2) Secondly, it was considered that both Gdańsk and Gdynia have enough issues in common that inter-port variation in the use of strategic management can be attributed to individuality rather than to the vagaries of geographical location or historical accident. Their hinterlands overlap extensively, the distances to the major European hub ports (e.g. Hamburg, Rotterdam, Bremerhaven, Antwerp and Dunkerque) and their Baltic competitors (e.g. Rostock, Tallinn, St Petersburg, Kaliningrad and those of southern Finland) are effectively identical. They differ only marginally in the commodities that are handled, port facilities provided and the infrastructural links with their hinterlands. Szczecin-Świnoujście, on the other hand, has always enjoyed a different and privileged position due to its geographical location. Until the end of the Second World War as the German "Port of Stettin", it was traditionally the main port for the then capital, Berlin. After 1945 it became the (Baltic Sea) port for landlocked Czechoslovakia. Meanwhile, via the Odra it has always been connected to the west European inland waterways and associated markets, a connection which is being developed again today (Kuzma 1997, Szwankowski 1994). Thus, its exclusion from this study is justified.

Objectivity It was mentioned above that questions may arise regarding the objectivity of answers to soft (qualitative) questions. As regards the evaluation of the benefits which strategic management can bring (question O), here subjectivity was a central issue and is actually a desired characteristic of both the question and answer as an opinion was the desired result. However, in other cases, attempts were made to obtain as much information upon a topic from as many sources (e.g. other persons or publications) as possible. For strategic research, the question of the reliability of the soundness of single respondent methods has been raised by Bowman and Ambrosini (1997). They found that there was no significant correlation between statements made by various organisational members of the same level and hence one must question their validity.[1] They suggest that single respondent techniques are sound when chief executives and other senior managers are not asked about the strategies undertaken - where they are

---

[1] Only in 1% of the cases examined was a scientific satisfying 0.8 Gronbach alpha value obtained.

likely to be biased since they alone designed them - but rather about intended strategies. Even if one were to question common research practice, in this study the respondents, with one exception had not been actively involved in designing strategies. Concerns regarding lack of objectivity in the results can therefore be dismissed with some confidence.

Generalisability First of all, this study is essentially a qualitative study and as such only concepts developed through the interpretation of data can be subject to generalisation. However, the standards used in this study to determine the elements of the ports' particular process of strategy-making are those used by strategic management literature at large. Therefore, any model or concept derived from this study can be applied immediately and tested in virtually any strategic management context including the wide variety of port strategy contexts that exist both within the East European region and elsewhere around the world.

Conduct of interviews

Interviews carry the particular disadvantage that they rely upon the respondent's willingness to give an insight into the issues under discussion. The degree of willingness depends upon many factors, some of which may be highly subconscious - Bailey speaks of interviews as a secondary social relationship (1987:178). The interviewer assured confidentiality in an attempt to create an atmosphere of trust. It was additionally stressed that the study was to analyse the Polish case in relation to the specific Polish environment and - very important - that comparisons with Western management systems were not intended and would not be made.

In addition, the knowledge and skills of the interviewer will always play a vital role in affecting the validity and usability of the results. Here the viewpoint of much of the research literature was shared by the research team In effect, the more the interviewer is informed about the subjects of the enquiry the better the interview results will always be. As a result, the interviewer drew upon extensive interview experience gained in a number of earlier research projects and also followed the research literature's general rules upon how to conduct an interview in general and semi-structured interviews in particular.

Questionnaire design

In view of the recommendations of research literature generally given regarding the design of self-completed questionnaires (Converse and Presser 1986 as referenced in Robson 1993:249), the following design issues were of relevance for this study and taken fully into consideration:

Question types

Closed and specific questions instead of open, general ones were used to increase standardisation.

Question order

In the absence of specific rules established by research (Robson 1993), here the approach was to start with general questions - formalia (A) and origin of strategy (B) - then to follow along with issues relating to the elements of the strategy process and finally to conclude with the personal evaluation of strategic management by the respondent (O). If this rule was broken (N. Organisational Culture) then this was because this topic may have been considered delicate by the respondent and thus new considerations had to be applied. In this case, transfer of the question to the end of the interview often seemed more appropriate.

Scaling of answers

In general, the intensity of the response was measured on a scale that included five categories (ranging from 1 to 5). Research evidence suggests that about one fifth of respondents tend to use the middle response option. To eliminate this bias, "yes-no" type questions alone could have been asked. However, in order to retain a sufficient breadth within the research questioning and to obtain and then retain the valuable information towards which direction non-committed respondents tended to incline (Robson 1993:248), a scale of five was chosen keeping the extreme options available (1 and 5) and allowing for rather less definite opinions (within the scores of 2 and 4).

In one case (F2), a "yes-no" question was asked because an intensity measure in this case was not needed. To allow an option for those respondents who were lacking knowledge upon the question at hand or who were very unsure about the issue, the questionnaire included a neutral no-opinion option.

Wording

In order to minimise subject error on the side of the non-English-native respondents, simple English was used deliberately. To exclude any errors in the survey caused by ignorance of management specific terminology, strategic management concepts were described in every-day language. The scientific reader may consult the questionnaire annotations in the appendix section later in this text for details of the technical terminology which was used.

Summary

This chapter started by discussing the conceptual models relevant to the research and then continued to illustrate how the target respondent group was determined and why for this particular qualitative study, the method of a questionnaire with closed-ended questions - either filled in by respondents alone or during a semi-structured interview - was the most appropriate way to collect primary data. It was also shown that extensive care and precautions in the design of the questionnaire as well as in the conduct of the interview, were taken to guarantee validity, objectivity and generalisability of the results.

5. Analysis

Introduction

This chapter presents the results of the field research. As was pointed out in the previous chapter, several port officials who it would have been preferable to interview, refused to participate in the survey whilst others were only willing to participate in semi-structured interviews. However, information regarding hard questions such as those relating to mission statements, commonly could be obtained from company documentation. Since this information is necessary for the reader to follow the discussion in the subsequent chapter, it will be presented in this chapter together with the results of the interviews and questionnaires. Where this type of source material has been used it will be indicated. It would have been possible to incorporate much of this information in Chapter 3 which analysed the two Polish ports of Gdynia and Gdańsk. However, it seemed more appropriate to progress logically through the order of the questions - rather than divide the detail observed between the two Chapters and thus break up the logical stream of the information.

Question A: Formalia

The Baltic Container Terminal in Gdynia (BCT) is organised into the three (functional) departments of "Marketing and Sales", "Operations and Technical Matters" and "Finance". A director heads each department and together they form the board of the BCT. The commercial director is at the same time President of the Board. Stevedoring, terminal operations, warehousing as well as container handling are part of the operations sub-department. Maintenance of the 38 gantries and the other equipment is undertaken by the sub-department entitled "Operations and Technical Matters".

It is a major aim of the Baltic Container Terminal that the "Operations and Technical Matters" department should be restructured during 1997 or at least by 1998. Whereas gantries and other handling equipment will be incorporated into the operations section, technical maintenance will rest with the technical department. The latter will be transformed into a private company which, to begin with, will continue to work for the Terminal but is eventually expected to acquire customers external to the port. This process of restructuring is being undertaken with the aim of increasing the overall profitability of the BCT.

Before the transformation process, the president of the company crafted the strategy for the terminal in conjunction with its three departments (commerce, operations, finance). Today, the hierarchy level represented within the BCT remains three whilst around 550 staff are employed. The number of departments increased directly after the transformation process: marketing and finance was now the responsibility of the terminal instead of the port authority - thus increasing the levels of strategic hierarchies that exist.

The General Cargo Terminal also took over responsibility for its finance and marketing after the transformation period. Its "Productions" department is organised according to products/shipping lines whilst a further sub-department exists for bonded warehouse services.

It was shown earlier in this paper that both port authorities chose a functional structure in their strategic management process.

Gdynia port officials emphasised that it was unclear what organisational changes will take place under the new Port Act. It was indicated that the present port authority will be eliminated and an entirely new port authority set up. It was also thought highly likely that Port Transport Limited, which is responsible for the transport within the port boundaries, and Port Supply Limited, responsible mainly for the port supplies process, will be eliminated with their services to be performed by outside (private) contractors. The number of employees in the port has dropped from around 7,000 in the 1970's to around 4,500 in 1997. The total number of staff employed by the port authority altogether, including non-port related employees, was not known since the port authority still operates a number of hotels, holiday resorts and a medical centre which are organised on a completely separate basis.

Question B: Generation of strategy

Strategies in the BCT are mainly designed and generated by senior internal experts. If external consultants are asked for their opinion then it is by invitation of the Terminal and not forced upon management by investors or other stakeholders. The general strategic direction was said to have been set at the beginning of the transformation process and continues largely unchanged to this day. This suggests a serious strategy continuum (see Chapter 2). In the Baltic Container Terminal, strategies do not evolve organically, they are deliberately designed. However, these designed strategies are subject to review if changes in the external environment demand that this should occur.

Officials of the Gdynia Port Authority indicated that several major development plans which have been recently undertaken, were drawn up by external experts including as an example, the Rotterdam Maritime Group. However, it was not possible to determine for certain, whether strategy in general is also mainly developed by non-port external strategists.

As regards the strategy of privatisation and structural ownership transformation, the need for the strategy was clearly imposed upon the port authority from outside, and the Treasury/Ministry of Transport in particular. However, how it was to be implemented was largely at the discretion of the individual Polish port. This strategy of privatisation, at least in the Port of Gdynia, has been developed incrementally.

Question C: The process of strategy development

This question - which was deliberately phrased in every-day language - enquired about the strategic management system currently used by the respondents. The BCT for example, applies strategic (posture) management and not strategic planning. Which system the other terminal operators and the port authorities apply, unfortunately was not clear from the discussions with them - suggesting a number of issues and a level of confusion relating to strategic choice and implementation and the priority that it holds within the organisational process of the ports.

Question D: Hierarchy of strategic planning

As was the case before the transformation process took place, strategies in the BCT are generally initiated and formulated by the senior management individuals (characteristic of top-down planning). Whereas before the period of transformation a single individual (the President) was responsible for crafting a strategy for the organisation, it is now normally the Board of Directors jointly together who undertake this task. Meanwhile, officials of the Baltic General Cargo Terminal (BTDG) were of the opinion that today's managers do not perform purely executive tasks any more. Rather, they are the creators of strategy whose task is to involve the lower levels of the organisation within the strategy formulation process when, or if, convenient or necessary. The port authority in Gdynia in contrast, takes the view that strategy formulation is a task of the senior management alone and thus makes no attempt to involve other parts of the organisation.

All officials in Gdynia shared the opinion that the port authority determines the mission and objectives for the whole port. Within this framework the operating companies are free to decide to do and to proceed as they wish. In an attempt to ensure that there is a strict policy of co-ordination for strategies, both terminal and port authority directors meet regularly for round-the-table discussions.

Academic respondents to the survey, familiar with the situation in Gdańsk said that the port authority - which is a landlord authority - also determines the mission and goals for the whole port but seems to have more influence than in the case of Gdynia, as a response to the problems of highly restricted and finite capital resources faced by the operating companies in the new economic environment.

Question E: Formality of planning

The officials of the BCT maintained they had a mission, Terminal objectives and detailed budgets written down for internal use but not for external consumption. In a similar fashion, the BTDG and the Gdynia Port Authority have formal objectives and budgets which are only communicated internally.

Question F: Mission statement

With one exception respondents refused to answer the question "What business is the company in?". The officials of the BCT stated that their aim was to "establish as many regular lines as possible". Meanwhile the *Port Handbook 1996/97* (1996:17) states that the BCT, "is poised to capitalise on its position as Poland's undisputed leader in box handling with ambitious plans to expand its facilities to meet an upsurge in demand for more capacity".

The content of the mission statement of the BCT was influenced by both the government and the port authority. Despite the excessively turbulent environment, the mission of the BCT has stayed the same. Mission statements were considered to be of considerable use for ports and although BCT's mission statement had not led to better co-operation among management since only three individuals are involved in the strategy process, it had improved internal communications and it was felt as a result, company performance.

Officials of the Gdynia Port Authority questioned the use of mission statements. In their experience potential customers tend to visit the site and inspect the service and facilities before making business decisions rather than be over influenced by the existence of a mission statement or whatever its content may be.

The Gdańsk WOC states for its Port Free Zone (1997a) that its mission is

"... to attract trade and business activity of the Port of Gdańsk by offering potential business partners the financial benefits of deferred payment customs duties, excise tax and VAT; [to create] the place in which most current techniques and technologies breaking new grounds in customer service and operations efficiency are implemented".

Question G: Internal analysis

The directors of the BCT regularly analyse the internal situation of their terminal in terms of its structure, the functions carried out and the organisational culture that has developed. The Gdynia port strategists use historical company data to determine the internal competitive position. However, whether competency profiles were employed in other departments than those of the operations department, could not be determined from the information provided.

Question H: External analysis

When scanning the external environment, the BCT strategists commonly use the PEST-analysis. To analyse the external competitive industry environment Porter's five forces model is usually applied. Strategists in the port authority of Gdynia said they were assessing their position in relation to their competitors in terms of throughput and not so much in terms of market share which was not considered to be of so much significance. All authority officials stated that it was not only the ports of Hamburg, Antwerp, Bremerhaven and Rotterdam who were main competitors for Gdynia but that

increased number of directors. Even today, white collar workers still have to participate in the one "working Saturday" to demonstrate enterprise unity. A working Saturday was introduced since the Polish law requires blue collar workers to work 42 hours / week.

Question N: Control

To make sure the company achieves its strategic objectives, the BCT regularly reviews their implementation system. Other, less frequently used methods are to control operational performance, to review the control system itself and to review the content of strategy. As regards the other companies, no information could be obtained to guide the researchers on conclusions for this issue.

Question O: Evaluation of strategic tools and techniques

In the BCT, officials feel that strategy is a vital issue and not just a luxury. They claim that it has a strong impact in forcing them into a logical approach to decision-making. However, senior level management spends about 70% of its time upon strategy-making which is less than before privatisation. In the General Cargo Terminal strategy was considered important, a view also shared by Port Authority officials.

Summary

This chapter presented the summarised results of the field research. Chapter Six will go on to contain a discussion of the findings and then proceed to assess the significance of the strategic management issues and decision processes for Polish ports in the coming years.

6. Discussion of the issues

Introduction

Chapter Six links the findings of the study with the knowledge generated in the theoretical chapters and tests the hypotheses presented in Chapter One.

Discussion

Four main issues clearly stand out from the analysis that has been conducted in the earlier chapters:

(1) In all cases, the respondents' first words were effectively that "strategy was a difficult topic" since the ports were in the middle of the tumultuous process of privatisation. This helps to indicate the far-reaching impacts of the transformation process in the Polish maritime sector.

(2) Secondly, strategy was always understood as "the set of actions taken to thrive in the future", i.e. it was always defined in terms of its content. However, since the strategists were all aware of at least part of their business environment, they also understood "strategy" at least in its dimension of (external) context.

(3) Enquiries regarding "strategy" were considered highly political (both internally and externally) and, curiously enough, were thus considered to be best put forward to the marketing department. Only in two cases were officials who

did not belong to the marketing department willing to convey their views on any of the issues put forward in the interviews or the questionnaires.

(4) The ghost of "a western port" was ever prevailing in the Polish port officials' minds. Without being asked, all respondents compared their organisations and actions with western ports and declared Poland still had a long way to go before their organisation, strategy or financial success matched those of the western European ports.

The elements of the strategy process

Mission Statements

Mission statements overall are not actively used in the ports' communication with outside stakeholders. The two strategic business units which did use mission statements both used them to define their customers, the service they aimed to provide, the geographical operating area that dominated their markets and the technology that they used. They also attempted to convey an organisational image for the port. In the port publications however, only one of the two mission statements was made to stand out by using an appropriate heading.

Audit

All respondents claimed to monitor the external environment. Since hardly any were able to describe the concepts they use it has to be concluded that environmental scanning is undertaken in a non-structured manner, relying rather upon experience than upon any true rationale. The same may be argued for the process of internal analysis where there was little tangible evidence of the process actually undertaken.

Generation of strategies, evaluation and choice

As regards how the two ports commonly generate strategic alternatives the picture still remains unclear. Only in one case was the port official able or willing to identify the decision criteria that were normally applied or the reasons for their choice.

Implementation and control

All ports, including the operating terminals are continuing to undergo significant organisational changes. These changes are of strategic nature and can be attributed to the effects of the ports' strategy towards transformation. From the data obtained it seems that no specific measures are taken to reduce either the gap between white and blue-collar workers or any general resistance to change that might exist. As regards the origin of strategy, it cannot be said whether strategies which were designed by outsiders are less easy or more difficult to implement due to a lack of problem ownership or commitment on the side of port employees. Also, it is not possible to determine whether imposed strategies face a higher level of resistance than the emerging ones.

Sequence and importance of the elements

Due to the low response rate, it is very difficult to reach conclusions regarding either the sequence or the importance of individual elements of the strategy process.

Tools and techniques used

Here data are also too few for us to make a generally reliable statement about which tools and techniques are favoured by the port strategists in the application of their strategies.

Perceived level of environmental turbulence

As was well illustrated in Chapter Three, Polish ports are operating in a highly turbulent business environment caused by changes within Poland itself as well as by changes occurring in other East European countries. At some point during the interviews, all respondents had expressed that they felt the environment was highly turbulent. However, when later asked to actively rate the four elements of turbulence according to the *impact upon the organisation*, turbulence was rated low. They would always try to use most up-to-date information from the most reliable sources, they claimed that they had effective systems to deal with the increased customer complexity and they had tried to learn from other leading ports of the world. There are two explanations for the gap between the objective and the perceived level of environmental turbulence. It may be possible that respondents wanted to convey the idea their business was in hand and thus they were operating a modern and competent organisation. It may also be possible that the four elements of turbulence lacked perceived sector importance[1], i.e. were not regarded as important to the business since the uncertainty caused by the process of privatisation and transformation was the dominating factor in decision-making and management.

Strategic management systems

A strategic management system is appropriate when it fits:

a) to the firm and;
b) to the environment.

In general, both the Port Authorities and the Gdynia operating subsidiaries can be seen to have transformed internally very slowly away from static, centralised, strict hierarchical organisations which practised top-down planning in functional departments into lean, more flexible and more democratic organisations. But they are yet by no means of a dynamic character. Here strategic (posture) management may be the upper limit of what will match with such organisations.

Firms operating in a highly turbulent environment like the Polish one, may be expected to apply a corresponding strategic management system, i.e. one which ranks high on Ansoff's turbulence scale. On the one hand, a free market economy has been introduced to Poland but so far, for a relatively short period of time. As a consequence, it is thus reasonable to expect that the chosen strategic system will be located rather at the bottom end of Ansoff's scale. However, following Obloj and Howard's (1996) research findings, it may be expected that Polish ports are also quick learners and use strategy at a medium level. Characteristic of such strategic (posture) systems is that capabilities are planned and change is managed. This, in turn, requires awareness about these issues. Such an awareness was however, found in one case only.

---

[1] Elenkov (1997) uses Daft et al.'s (as referenced in Elenkov 1997) terminology to express that only uncertainty of a factor, which is perceived as having impact on the firm, is regarded as actual strategic uncertainty by an organisation.

Testing of the hypotheses

In the view of these findings it can be said that:

Hypothesis one: *The ports of Gdynia and Gdańsk are expected to apply a process of strategy-making where all steps of the classical model are employed in sequential order* cannot be supported. For the port authorities of Gdańsk and Gdynia only limited data were available. Only for the BCT (Gdynia) was sufficient data available to come to the conclusion that at least some elements of the classical model are employed.

Hypothesis two: *The ports of Gdynia and Gdańsk are expected to have different strategic management systems and to apply different techniques and tools* can neither be verified nor dismissed given the information available although some differences in approach were apparent.

Hypothesis three: *The two ports are expected to apply a strategic management system for an environmental turbulence level of medium degree* can only be answered for the port of Gdynia. Strategic management systems at level three require by their nature that their applicants have a sound understanding of the strategic process. Since this was - with one exception - not the case, hypothesis three has to be generally dismissed.

Summary

In this chapter we have outlined an analysis of the changing strategic management approaches adopted in Polish ports and recognised the speed and direction of change which is influencing the marketplace. The problems of collecting primary data have been acknowledged and hopefully sufficiently overcome to reach some interesting and useful conclusions. In the final chapter, we shall reach some tentative conclusions on the developments in strategic management that have been and continue to take place in the Polish ports sector.

7. Conclusions

Summary of the study

This research investigated the topical and unique question of how the two major Polish ports of Gdynia and Gdańsk, which operate in a highly turbulent environment, use strategic management to meet present competition in its market in order not only to survive but to prosper into the 21st century. The focus of this exploratory field study were two of the three dimensions of strategy: that is, strategic context and strategic process.

The purpose of this research was to determine the elements of the process of strategy-making in the two ports, to classify their strategic management systems in terms of correlation with the level of perceived environmental turbulence and to explain any inter-port variations, if any, in the light that both ports are experiencing very largely, the same environmental influences in very similar physical locations.

It was shown that the process of strategy-making consists of elements of mission, audit, the generation of strategy, evaluation and choice, and implementation and control. Depending upon the business type of the organisation, specific elements may be more or less important. The benefits of strategic management can be enjoyed by the port industry as well as other commercial sectors even though it has been little applied anywhere in the world. This is independent of public or private ownership.

Various tools are available for the strategist and it was suggested that only a few should be applied and these core tools, namely those reflecting environmental dynamics and covering all steps of the strategic process, are essential for effecting strategic formulation.

The turbulence of the environment in which the ports of Gdynia and Gdańsk operate was and is caused by the transformation of Poland and other East European countries from centrally planned into free market economies. An unstable economic situation within Poland and a change of the trade flows in Eastern Europe poses severe strain upon Polish ports. Additionally, the traditional hinterland of the Polish ports has been and continues to be eroded so that Gdynia and Gdańsk not only face intra-port and inter-Polish competition but now compete also with other modes of transport as well as with foreign (Baltic and West European) ports.

An analysis of the primary data, which were obtained through semi-structured interviews of port strategists in combination with closed-ended questionnaires, revealed that respondents primarily think in terms of strategic content when they refer to "strategy". The organisations have not yet started to investigate the process of internal strategy-making they use by themselves. In addition, strategy-making was often considered as highly political and several respondents felt "strategically" incompetent and inadequate in comparison with western and Asian companies and ports which hindered their ability and willingness to comment.

As regards the process of strategy-making, the findings of the study suggest that this process is rather unstructured and hardly formalised in Polish ports. This may be due to the fact that only few individuals are currently involved in crafting the strategies. Only a few strategic tools were used, if information was obtainable at all. It could not be determined whether strategic planning, strategic posture management or real-time systems were favoured. The lack of data also prevented any truly detailed inter-port comparison.

Recommendations

As the heading indicates, this is the section where the discussion is traditionally taken one step further onto a normative level.

In the context of this study this would imply that at this stage we should be indicating:

> a) the ideal extent to which strategic management is to be employed in Polish ports and possibly in Eastern European ports more generally; and
> b) the ideal strategic management process and system in relation to the degree of environmental turbulence experienced in Polish ports.

To *examine* the present situation, the yardstick of traditional concepts of strategic management were used. If we were to take these as a yardstick for the *ideal*, we indeed would find that Polish ports have not yet anywhere nearly approached exhaustion of the possibilities. It was illustrated in Chapter 2 that strategic management is subject to a continuing evolutionary process. Thus, does non-adherence to a current, (in western business cultures) well-practised strategic management system mean their own practised system should be changed? Raison d'emploi of strategic management, certainly, is the achievement of a competitive advantage and this suggests that this is the case as a result. However, we should remember that the ports sector worldwide is hardly an advanced user of strategic management models and thus the Polish situation is perhaps not quite as poor as might first be considered.

Here a concept could be adopted which was conveyed by almost all respondents during interviews: the idea of "western" standards being imposed which had to be accepted to obtain finance and attract investors.

From this point of view, why not adopt the same lens? Why not beat the enemy at his own game? A start could be an increased application of strategic management to the customer interface of the organisation, using mission statements to *convey* to outsiders that the organisation *is* undertaking long-term thinking - even if it isn't. This, in turn, would communicate stability to potential investors which additionally, might attract the foreign investment so desperately needed.

In a second step, the port strategist may want to increase the use of strategic management internally. This could begin with the use of few core strategic management tools such as basic financial control, an active marketing framework, and building an organisational culture that is suitable. Ports like that of Singapore prove that this is possible and worthwhile.

Obloj and Howard (1996) maintain that successful Polish firms chose breakthrough strategies rather than incremental change. This may be true for manufacturing companies like Ambra S.A or even shipyards. Ports, however, are in a different situation. They can only to a very limited degree change their service range without losing their identity as a port. However, does this matter and is it not what has happened in west European ports already?

As discussed earlier, strategic management is about identifying key factors and making clear strategic choices. This suggests that the application of any type of strategic management may, as a side effect, further sharpen management's view towards relevance and focus. An outcome of this process may well be the decision to create a port which specialises in certain commodities, a trend which can be observed in all major ports of the world[2] and which has been suggested for Polish ports as well.

Increasing strategic management is talking "cross-culturally" on a business systems level. Adopting a lens used by western investors is like learning a new foreign language: facilitating communication and in the particular case of Gdynia and Gdańsk may result in attracting foreign investment.

Recommendations for further study and some conclusions

At this concluding stage it would be helpful to indicate where future research efforts should be concentrated. First of all it would be desirable to undertake the survey again at a later date in the future. The objective would be to determine whether the awareness for and the use of strategic management has increased. Indicators would be; a higher response rate; and facilitated interviews in that respondents would not only themselves differentiate between content, process and context, but also feel more confident to answer questions.

The process of transformation towards privatisation is still ongoing and further changes in the strategic management system are bound to occur. Therefore this study will remain highly topical for some time. When the chaos and disruption caused by the privatisation process has ebbed away, management will sail through calmer waters and it can be expected that strategic management, together with other western management techniques, will then become increasingly important.

For researchers with an interest in marketing, Polish ports provide a topical and fertile field for further investigation. Here it may be suggested that the inclusion of the third main Polish port of Szczecin-Świnoujście in the study, would be particularly useful. Extension to minor ports within Poland - e.g. Ustka, Kołobrzeg, Darłowo and Łeba would provide further interesting results whilst the possibilities of taking the structure to ports in other Eastern European countries - e.g. Varna and Bourgas in Bulgaria, Constantza in Romania, Tallinn in Estonia and St Petersburg and Kaliningrad in Russia - should not be overlooked.

And yet another and final challenge remains: designing a model which combines objective measures for the level of environmental turbulence with an impact analysis of external factors influencing the Polish maritime industry.

References

American Association of Port Authorities (AAPA) (1988), *Strategic planning: A guide for the port industry*, Alexandria VA: AAPA.

Ansoff, H. I. (1965), *Corporate strategy*, New York: McGraw-Hill.

Ansoff, H. I. (1991), Critique of Henry Mintzberg's the design school: reconsidering the basic premises of strategic management, *Strategic Management Journal*, vol. 12, pp. 449-461.

Ansoff, H. I. and McDonnell, E. J. (1990), *Implanting strategic management*, 2nd ed. London: Prentice Hall.

Arlt, W. H. (1987), Information requirements in strategic planning in the ports industry: specification and management of a data base, *Maritime Policy and Management,* vol. 14, no. 1, pp. 49-61.

Bailey, K. D. (1987), *Methods of social research*, 3rd ed. London: The Free Press.

Baker, C. (1997), Battle for the east, *Port development International*, March, pp.29-31.

Baltic Container Terminal (1996 and 1997), *BCT*. Unpublished internal company publication (in Polish and English).

Baltic Container Terminal (1996), *BCT*, Company publication.

Blaxter, L., Hughes, C. and Tight, M. (1996), *How to research*, Buckingham: Open University Press.

Boswell, J. S. (1983), *Business policies in the making*, London: George, Allen and Unwin.

Bowman, C. and Asch, D. (1996), *Managing strategic change*, London: McMillan Press.

Boyle, D. (ed.) (1991), *Strategic service management*, Oxford: Pergamon Press.

Branch, A. E. (1986), *Elements of port operation and management*, London: Chapman and Hall.

Campbell, A. and Yeung, S. (1991), Brief case: mission, vision and strategic intent, *Long Range Planning*, vol. 24 no. 4, pp. 145-147.

Campbell, A. and Yeung, S. (1991), Creating a sense of mission, *Long Range Planning*, vol. 24 no. 4, pp. 10-20.

Campbell, A., Devine, M. and Young, D. (1990), *A sense of mission*, London: Financial Times/Pitman.

Chadwick, G. (1981), *A systems view of planning*, 2nd ed. Oxford: Pergamon Press.

Challinor, D. (1996). Baltic bridge, *Port Development International*, vol. 12 no. 6, pp. 35-39.

Chandler, A. D. (1970), *Strategy and structure*, Boston: Harvard Business School Press.

Chasan, D. J. and Dowd, T. J. (1988), Strategic planning, in Hershman, M. (ed.) *Urban ports and harbour management*, New York: Taylor and Francis.

Christensen, C. R., Andrews, K. R., Bower, J. L., Hamermesh, R. G., and Porter, M. E. (1982), *Business policy: text and cases*, 5th ed. Homewood: Irwin.

David, F. R. (1989), How companies define their mission, *Long Range Planning*, vol. 22 no. 1, pp. 90-97.

David, F. R. (1995), *Strategic management*, 5th ed. New Jersey: Prentice-Hall..

de Witt, B. and Meyer, R. (1994), *Strategy - process, content, context, an international perspective*, Minneapolis: West Publishing Company.

Der grosse Duden - Fremdwoerterbuch (1966), 5th ed. Mannheim: Dudenverlag (in German).

Dobrowolski, K. and Szwankowski, S. (1997), *The influence of restructuring and privatisation of Polish sea ports on their competitiveness*. Unpublished.

Dobrowolski, K. (1994a), Structural and ownership transformation in Polish seaports and shipping enterprises, in University of Gdańsk (ed.) *Maritime transport during the transformation of Poland's economy*, pp. 27-37. Gdańsk: Institute of Maritime Transport Economics, University of Gdańsk.

Dobrowolski, K. (1994b), The privatizing of state-owned enterprises in Poland's economy, in University of Gdańsk and University of Rostock (eds.) *Processes of changes in ownership in maritime transport in Poland and East Germany*, pp. 13-24. Gdańsk: University of Gdańsk.

Drucker, P. F. (1974), *Management, task, responsibilities and practices*, New York: Harper and Row.

Drucker, P. F. (1989). What business can learn from nonprofits. *Harvard Business Review*, July/August, pp. 88-93.

Dutton, J. E. and Duncan, R. E. (1987). The influence of the strategic planning process on strategic change. *Strategic Management Journal*, vol. 8 no. 2, pp. 103-116.

Elenkov, D. S. (1997). Strategic uncertainty and environmental scanning: the case for institutional influences on scanning behaviour. *Strategic Journal of Management*, vol. 18 no. 4, pp. 287-302.

Engelhoff, W.G. (1993). Great strategy or great strategy implementation. *Sloan Management Review*, vol. 34 no. 2, pp. 37-50.

Fairplay (1997). Polish harvest, vol. 331, issue 5920, 29th May, p.48.

Faulkner, D. and Bowman, C. (1995). *The essence of competitive strategy*. London: Prentice Hall.

Feurer, R. and Chaharbaghi, K. (1994). Defining competitiveness: a holistic approach. *Management Decision*, vol. 32 no. 2, pp. 49-59.

Feurer, R. and Chaharbaghi, K. (1995). Strategy development: past, present and future. *Management Decision*, vol. 33 no. 6, pp. 11-21.

Filfield, P. and Gilligan, C. (1995). *Strategic marketing management*. Oxford: Butterworth Heinemann.

Flamholz, E. (1990). *Growing pains: how to make the transition from an entrepreneurship to a professionally managed firm*. San Francisco: Jossey-Bass.

Flamholz, E. (1995). Managing organizational transitions. *European Management Journal*, vol. 13 no. 1, pp. 39-51.

Frankel, E. G. (1989). Strategic planning applied to shipping and ports. *Maritime Policy and Management*, vol. 16 no. 2, pp. 123-132.

Freeman, R. E. and Lorange, P. (1985). Theory building in strategic management, in Lamb R. and Shrivastava P. (eds.) *Advances in strategic management*. Greenwich, Conn.: JAI Press.

Galbraith, J. R. and Kazanjian, R. K. (1986). *Strategy implementation*. 2nd ed. New York: West Publishing Co.

Galpin, T. J. (1997). Making strategy work. *Journal of Business Strategy*, vol. 18 no. 1, January/February, pp. 12-14.

Gdańsk Pomerania Development Agency and Provincial Governor's Office of Gdańsk (eds.) (1996). *Investing in the Gdańsk Province*, July. Gdańsk: Unilex.

Grant, R. M. (1985). *Contemporary strategy analysis*. 2nd ed. Oxford: Blackwell.

Gray, R. and Panayides, P.M. (1997). Marketing the professional ship management service. *Maritime Policy and Management*, vol. 24 no. 3, pp. 233-244.

Greenley, E. G. (1989). *Strategic management*. London: Prentice Hall.

Hall, D. (1992). East European ports in a restructured Europe, in Hoyle. B. S. and Pinder, D. A. (eds.) *European port cities in transition*. 6th ed. London: Behaven Press.

Hart, P., Ledger, G., Roe, M. and Smith, B. (1993). *Shipping policy in the European Community*. Aldershot: Avebury.

Hart, S. L. (1992). An integrative framework for strategy-making processes. *Academy of Management Review*, vol. 22 no. 1, pp. 327-351.

Hofer, C. W. and Schendel, D. (1978). *Strategy formulation: analytical concepts*. New York: West Publishing Co.

Hussey, D. (1978). Portfolio analysis: practical experience with the DPM. *Long Range Planning*, vol. 11 no. 4.

International Financial Statistics Yearbook 1995 (1995). vol. xlviii. Washington: IMF.

International Financial Statistics Yearbook 1997 (1997). vol. l no. 5. May. Washington: IMF.

Jackson, T. (1997). Dare to be different - The management interview: Michael Porter. *Financial Times*, 19 June.

Jacobs, T. (1997). Punctuated equilibrium: the Burton Group in Johnson, G. and Scholes, K. (eds.) *Exploring corporate strategy*. 4th ed. London: Prentice Hall.

Jauch, L. R. and Glueck, W. F. (1988). *Strategic management and business policy*. 4th ed. New York: McGraw-Hill.

Johnson, G. (1988). Rethinking incrementalism. *Strategic Management Journal*, vol. 9 no. 1, pp. 75-91.

Johnson, G. and Scholes, K. (1997). *Exploring corporate strategy*. 4th ed. London: Prentice Hall.

Karloef, B. (1989). *Business strategy - a guide to concepts and models*. London: McMillan Press Ltd.

Koontz, H. and Weihrich, H. (1990). *Essentials of Management*. 5th ed. New York: Mc Graw-Hill.

Kuzma, L. (1994a). Restructuralizing and privatizing of Poland's sea ports, in University of Gdańsk and University of Rostock (eds.) *Processes of changes in ownership in maritime transport in Poland and East Germany*. pp. 35-44. Gdańsk: University of Gdańsk.

Kuzma, L. (1994b). *Restrukturisierung und Privatisierung der Haefen von Gdańsk und Gdynia* [Restructurisation and privatisation of the ports of Gdańsk and Gdynia]. Unpublished (in German).

Kuzma, L. (1996). *Die Transformationsprozesse in den polnischen Seehaefen in den Jahren 1991-1995* [The transformation process in Polish seaports in 1991-1995]. Unpublished lecture at the University of Rostock, October (in German).

Kuzma, L. (1997). *Polnische Seehaefen auf dem Markt der Hafenleistungen im Ostseeraum* [Polish seaports in the market of port services in the Baltic Sea region]. Unpublished lecture at the University of Rostock, October (in German).

Ledger, G. and Roe, M. (1993). East European shipping and economic change: a conceptual model. *Maritime Policy and Management*, vol. 20. no. 3, pp. 229-241.

Ledger, G. and Roe, M. (1993). Polish privatisation. *Lloyd's Shipping Economist*, vol. 15 no. 4, pp. 6-8.

Ledger, G. and Roe, M. (1996). *East European change and shipping policy*. Aldershot: Avebury.

Leuthesser, L. and Kohli, C. (1997). Corporate identity: the role of mission statements. *Business Horizons*, vol. 40, May/June, pp. 59-66.

Lipton, M. (1996). Demystifying the development of an organizational vision. *Sloan Management Review*, vol. 37 no. 4, pp. 83-92.

Lloyd's List (1989). Gdańsk aims to be main import centre. 12 December.

Lloyd's List (1989). Gdynia seeks approval for major changes in structure and ownership. 12 December.

Lloyd's List (1994). Gdynia on privatisation road. 2 September.

Lloyd's List (1994). New Port Act will define privatisation process. 2 September.

Lloyd's List (1995). Gdańsk sees future in bulk. 26 May.

Lloyd's List (1995). Gdynia faces key stage in growth. 26 May.

Lloyd's List (1995). Maritime sector enjoys economic success after restructuring. 26 May.

Lloyd's List (1996). Coal crisis hits Gdańsk port handling results. 27 June.

Lloyd's List (1996). Containers boost Gdynia. 27 June.

Lloyd's List (1997). Centralised structure will soon be ended. 29 May.

Lloyd's List (1997). Gdańsk throughput falls by nearly 10%. 29 May.

Lloyd's List (1997). Gdynia celebrates in style. 29 May.

Lloyd's List (1997). Major port and yards changes spur maritime sector debate. 29 May.

Martinsons, M. G. (1993). Strategic innovation: a lifeboat for planning in turbulent waters. *Management Decision*, vol. 31 no. 8, pp. 4-11.

McNamee, P. B. (1992). *Strategic management*. Oxford: Butterworth-Heinemann Ltd.

Meyer, C. (1993). *Fast cycle time*. New York: Free Press.

Miller, D. and Friesen, P. (1980). Momentum and evolution in organisational adaption. *Academy of Management Journal*, vol. 23, no. 4, pp. 591-614.

Miller, D. C. (1983). *Handbook of research design and social measurement*. 4th ed. London: Longman.

Mintzberg, H. (1976). Planning on the left side and managing on the right. *Harvard Business Review*, July/August, pp. 56.

Mintzberg, H. (1984). *Of strategies, deliberate and emergent. Readings in strategic management*. Milton Keynes: Oxford University Press.

Mintzberg, H. (1990a). Strategy formulation: schools of thought, in Frederickson, J. W. (ed.) *Perspectives on strategic management*. New York: Harper and Row.

Mintzberg, H. (1990b). The Design School. *Strategic Management Journal*, March, pp. 171-195.

Mintzberg, H. (1991). Learning 1, Planning 0. *Strategic Management Journal*, September, pp. 463-466.

Mintzberg, H. (1994a). Rethinking strategic planning; part I: pitfalls and fallacies. *Long Range Planning*, vol. 27 no. 3, June pp. 12-21.

Mintzberg, H. (1994b). Rethinking strategic planning; part II: new roles for planners. *Long Range Planning*, vol. 27 no. 3, June pp. 22-30.

Mintzberg, H. (1994c).The fall and rise of strategic planning. *Harvard Business Review*, January/February, pp. 107-114.

Mintzberg, H. (1994d). *The rise and fall of strategic planning*. Hemel Hempstead: Prentice Hall International Ltd.

Mintzberg, H. and Quinn, J. B. (1996). *The strategy process*. 3rd ed. London: Prentice Hall.

Mintzberg, H. and Waters, J. (1985). Of strategies, deliberate and emergent. *Strategic Management Journal*, July/September, vol. 6 no. 3, pp. 257-272.

Misztal, K. (1994a). Polish seaports in the context of the association agreement between Poland and the EC, in University of Antwerp and University of Gdańsk (eds.) *IV. The EC and Poland - regulation of maritime transport*. pp. 33-42. Gdańsk: University of Gdańsk.

Misztal, K. (1994b). Systems transformations in Poland's seaports, in University of Gdańsk and University of Rostock (eds.) *Processes of changes in ownership in maritime transport in Poland and East Germany*. pp. 25-34. Gdańsk: University of Gdańsk.

Misztal, K. (1996). The place of Polish sea ports in the Baltic Sea basin, in Institut fuer Verkehr und Logistik, Rostocker Beitraege zur Verkehrswissenschaft und Logistik Heft 5: *Market transition and structural changes in shipping and ports of Baltic Sea countries*. pp. 117-124. Rostock: Universitaet Rostock (in German and English).

Misztal, K.(1993). *The present state and future prospects of Polish sea ports*. Turku: University of Turku.

Misztal, K., Szwankowski, S. and Wasilewska, K. (1997). *Problems of developing land-sea transport infrastructure for handling Polish foreign trade and transit.* Gdańsk: University of Gdańsk (in Polish and English).

Moore, S. (1995). Making sense of strategic management: towards a constructive guide. *Management Decision*, vol. 33 no 1, pp. 19-23.

Morton, M. S. (1995). Emerging organizational forms for the 21st century. *European Management Journal*, vol. 13 no. 4, pp. 339-345.

Mundy, M. (1995). Market makers. *Port Development International*, Freight Europe Supplement, vol. 11 no. 6, pp. F9-F11.

Neuman, W. L. (1994). *Social research methods.* 2nd ed. Boston: Allyn and Bacon.

Nicholls, J. (1995). The MCC decision matrix. *Management Decision*, vol. 33 no. 6, pp. 4-10.

NU comission economique pour l'europe (1995). *Bulletin annuel de statistiques des transports pour l'europe et l'amerique du nord 1995*, tom. xlv. Geneve: United Nations.

Obloj, K. and Howard, T. (1996). Breaking away from the past: strategies of successful Polish firms. *European Journal of Management*, vol. 14 no. 5, pp. 467-476.

Pearce, J. A. and Robinson, R. B. (1994). *Strategic management: formulation, implementation, and control.* 5th. ed. Burr Ridge, Illinois: Irwin.

Perry, L. T., Stott, R. G. and Smallwood, W. N. (1993). *Real-time strategy - improvising team based planning for a fast-changing world.* New York: John Wiley and Sons.

Pettigrew, A. (1988). *The management of strategic change.* Oxford: Basil Blackwell.

Piercy, N. F. (1995). Marketing and strategy fit together. *Management Decision*, vol. 33 no. 1, January, pp. 42-47.

Piercy, N. F. and Morgan, N. A. (1994). Mission analysis: an operational approach. *Journal of General Management*, vol. 19 no. 3, Spring, pp. 1-19

Polish Maritime Industry Journal (1992). Downturn in transit business from Polish ports, vol. 2 no. 1, p. 30.

Polish Maritime Industry Journal (1992). Port of Gdynia aims to attract new lines and cargo, vol. 2 no. 2, p. 31.

Polish Maritime Industry Journal (1993). Port of Gdynia: 70 years of progress, vol. 3 no. 1, p. 34.

Polish Maritime Industry Journal (1994). Port of Gdańsk requires finance for privatisation, vol. 4 no. 1, p. 33.

Polish Maritime Industry Journal (1994). Port of Gdynia now restructuring, vol. 4 no. 1, p. 32.

Port Gdynia Handbook 1996-97 (1996). Ardleigh: Land and Marine Publications Ltd.

Porter, M. E. (1980). *Competitive strategy*. New York: Free Press.

Porter, M. E. (1985). *Competitive advantage - creating and sustaining superior performance*. New York: Free Press.

Porter, M. E. (1990). *Competitive strategy: techniques for analyzing industries and competitors*. New York: The Free Press.

Porter, M. E. (1996). What is strategy? *Harvard Business Review*, November/December, pp. 61-78.

Press and Information Department of the Embassy of the Republic of Poland (1997). *General Information*. Unpublished document, September 8.

Robson, C. (1993). *Real world research*. Oxford: Blackwell.

Roe, M. (ed.) (1997). *Shipping in the Baltic region*. Aldershot: Avebury.

Roe, M. (1998) *Commercialisation in the Baltic Maritime Marketplace*. Aldershot: Avebury.

Romanelli, E. and Tushmann, M. L. (1994). Organisational transformation as punctuated equilibrium. *Academy of Management Journal*, vol. 37, no. 9, pp. 1141-1161.

Rosen, R. (1995). *Strategic management*. London: Pitman.

Rydzkowski, W. and Wojewodzka-Krol, K. (1997). Selected issues in Poland's transport policy in the 1990's. *Transport i logistyka*, vol. 5, pp. 55-67, Sopot: University of Gdańsk.

Schendel, D. E. and Hofer, C. W. (1979). *Strategic management: a new view of business policy and planning*. Boston: Little Brown.

Senge, P. (1990). The fifth discipline: the art and practice of the learning organisation. New York: Doubleday/Century.

Senge, P. (1994). *The fifth discipline: strategies and tools for building a learning organisation*. London: Brealey.

Shipman, M. (1988). *The limitations of social research*. 3rd ed. London: Longman.

Shipping World and Shipbuilder (1997). Area review: Poland and Baltic. Basingstoke: Marine Publications International Ltd, June, pp. 8-13.

Snow, C.C. and Thomas, J. B. (1994). Field research methods in strategic management: contributions to theory building and testing. *Journal of Management Studies*, vol. 31 no. 4, pp. 457-478.

Sokol, R. (1992). Simplifying strategic planning. *Management Decision*, vol. 30 no. 7, pp. 11-17.

Stalk, G. and Hout, T. (1990). *Competing against time*. New York: Free Press.

Stalk, G., Evans, P. and Shulman, L. E. (1992). Competing on capabilities: the new rules of corporate strategy. *Harvard Business Review*, March/April, pp. 57-69.

Statistisches Bundesamt and Eurostat (eds.) (1995). *Country profile Poland 1994*. Luxembourg: Office for Official Publications of the European Communities.

Sulima-Chlaszczak, K. (1994). Labour market in Polish sea ports during the transformation to the market economy, in University of Gdańsk (ed.) *Maritime transport during the transformation of Poland's economy*. pp. 51-64. Gdańsk: Institute of Maritime Transport Economics, University of Gdańsk.

Szwankowski, S. (1994). Polish seaports on the competitive market of transport services, in University of Gdańsk (ed.) *Maritime transport during the transformation of Poland's economy*. pp. 79-90. Gdańsk: Institute of Maritime Transport Economics, University of Gdańsk.

Szwankowski, S. (1996). Prospects of Polish transport corridors in the service of Baltic transport and trade, in Institut fuer Verkehr und Logistik, Rostocker Beitraege zur Verkehrswissenschaft und Logistik Heft 5: *Market transition and structural changes in shipping and ports of Baltic Sea countries*. pp. 125-132. Rostock: Universitaet Rostock (in German and English).

Szwankowski, S. and Tubielewicz, A. (1992). *Planowanie strategiczne w portach morskich* [Strategic planning in sea ports]. Gdańsk: Prace Instytut Morskiego (in Polish).

Tampoe, M. (1994). Exploiting the core competencies of your organization. *Long Range Planning*, vol. 27 no. 4 pp. 66-77.

Taylor, B. (1997). The return of strategic planning - once more with feeling. *Long Range Planning*, vol. 30 no. 3, pp. 334-344.

Taylor, Z. (1984). Seaport development and the role of the state: the case of Poland, in Hoyle, B. S. and Hilling, D. (eds.) Seaport systems and spatial change. Chichester: John Wiley and Sons.

The 1997 Guide to emerging currencies (1997). Euromoney, July. London: Euromoney Publications.

The Coastal Times (1997). Good and bad news about Scandinavian co-operation, no. 3 (45) March.

Thomas, B. J. (1994). Privatisation of UK seaports. *Maritime Policy and Management*, vol. 21 no. 2, pp. 135-148.

Thomas, B. J. (1994). The need for organisational change in seaports. *Maritime Policy and Management*, vol. 18 no. 1, pp. 69-78.

Thompson, J. L. (1997). Strategic management, awareness and change. 3rd ed. London: International Thomson Business Press.

Tubielewicz, A. (1994). *Kompleksowe zagospodarownie portu Gdańsk* [Complex development of the Port of Gdańsk]. Gdańsk: Instytut Morski (in Polish).

Tubielewicz, A. (1995). Restructuring and privatization of Polish sea ports. *Ports and Harbors*, vol. 40 no. 9, pp. 20-22.

Tubielewicz, A. (1997). *Strategy of the Gdańsk Port Authority.* (in Polish)

UNCTAD (1993). *Strategic planning for port authorities.* New York: UN.

Veliyath, R. and Shortell, S. M. (1993). Strategic orientation, strategic planning system characteristics and performance. *Journal of Management Studies*, vol. 30 no. 3, pp. 359-382.

Wasilewska, K. (1997). Poland on the Southern Baltic transit market, in Institut fuer Verkehr und Logistik (ed.), Rostocker Beitraege zur Verkehrswissenschaft und Logistik Heft 5: *Market transition and structural changes in shipping and ports of Baltic Sea countries.* pp.133-143. Rostock: Universitaet Rostock (in German and English).

Webster, J. L., Reif, W. E. and Bracker, J. S. (1989). The manager's guide to strategic planning tools and techniques. *Planning Review*, November/December.

Wilson, I. (1994). Strategic planning isn't dead - it changed. *Long Range Planning*, vol. 27 no. 4, pp. 12-24.

Wilson, R. M., Gilligan, C. T. and Pearson, D. (1992). *Strategic marketing management: planning implementation and control.* Oxford: Butterworth Heinemann.

Zarząd Portu Gdańsk (1996). *Port Handbook.*

Zarząd Portu Gdańsk (1997a). *Port Free Zone - General data.* Unpublished internal company document. Poland.

Zarząd Portu Gdańsk (1997b). *Port Free Zone.* Poland.

Zarząd Portu Gdańsk (1996). Duty Free Zone Gdańsk: Investment opportunities. *Welcome*, 15/48 November, p. 16.

Zielinski, A. (1997). The Gdynia Harbour. *Polish Market*, no. 8, pp. 34-35.

Bibliography

Berenyi I. (1996). *Poland. Government and shipping poles apart.* Seatrade Review, July.

Blazyca G. and Rapacki R. (eds) (1991). *Poland into the 1990s.* Pinter Publishers; London.

Breitzmann K.H. (1996). *Market transition and structural changes in shipping and ports of Baltic sea countries.* Institut für Verkehr und Logistik, Universität Rostock.

Breitzmann K.H. (ed.) (1994). *Shipping, ports and transport in transition to a market economy.* Institut für Verkehr und Logistik, Universität Rostock.

Business Central Europe (1997). *Slow death.* April.

Clayton R. (1994). Working without Warsaw. *Fairplay,* May 12.

COWIconsult (1995). *Strategic study of ports and maritime transport in the Baltic Sea.* European Union Regional Group on Ports and Maritime Transport in the Baltic Sea (unpublished).

Ernst and Young (1992). *Doing business in Poland.* Warsaw.

European Commission (1996). *EU relations with Poland.* Background Report B/10/96.

Fairplay (1996). Breaking up at POL. *Fairplay,* May 9.

Fairplay (1996). Home to roost. Russia's problems are Poland's gain. *Fairplay,* January 25.

Fairplay (1996). Poland. Excess of success. *Fairplay,* May 9.

Fairplay (1996). Poor connections. *Fairplay,* May 9.

Fairplay (1997). Gdynia takeover 'close'. *Fairplay,* February 27.

Financial Times (1996). *Polish promise.* September 13.

Financial Times (1996). *Polish service industries.* October 30.

Financial Times (1997). *Poland.* March 26.

International Freighting Weekly (1995). *Stena steams into Poland.* August 14.

Kierzkowski H., Okolski M. and Wellisz S. (eds) (1993). *Stabilization and structural adjustment in Poland.* Routledge; London.

Ledger G.D. and Roe M.S. (1995). Positional change in the Polish liner shipping market: a framework approach. *Maritime Policy and Management,* 22, 4, 295-318.

Linde H. and Tang L. (eds) (1991). *Cooperation and competition between east and west in maritime transport.* Papers presented at the Second International Conference on World Liner Shipping, Gdańsk.

Lloyd's List (1995). *Agency finding a big demand for Polish crew.* September 5.

Lloyd's List (1995). *New common feeder established by port.* September 5.

Lloyd's List (1995). *Poland. Special Report.* September 5.

Lloyd's List (1995). *Polish crew agents back trade lobby.* November 9.

Lloyd's List (1995). *Unity to expand services.* December 18.

Lloyd's List (1996). *Fleet remains on path to privatisation.* September 2.

Lloyd's List (1996). *POL's debt for equity plan.* February 8.

Lloyd's List (1997). *'Boomerang' arrives in the Baltic.* May 25.

Lloyd's List (1997). *Europort applies for terminal in Gdańsk.* May 25.

Lloyd's List (1997). *Gdańsk free zone proves popular.* July 17.

Lloyd's List (1997). *Gdańsk yard sale pending.* October 18.

Lloyd's List (1997). *Gdańsk yard wins backing for new vessel.* May 25.

Lloyd's List (1997). *Gdynia celebrates in style.* May 29.

Lloyd's List (1997). *Gdynia facility.* October 9.

Lloyd's List (1997). *Gdynia. Special report.* September 23.

Lloyd's List (1997). *IACS suspends Polish Register.* May 20.

Lloyd's List (1997). *Leader.* March 8.

Lloyd's List (1997). *Mitsui secures contract for five Polish Steamship bulk carriers.* October 16.

Lloyd's List (1997). *New look at ferry links with Poland.* May 26.

Lloyd's List (1997). *Poland revamps shipping registry.* October 14.

Lloyd's List (1997). *Poland. A special report.* September 24.

Lloyd's List (1997). *Polish Baltic move nearer to privatisation.* September 24.

Lloyd's List (1997). *Polish ferry privatisation.* August 9.

Lloyd's List (1997). *Polish ferry traffic up.* October 18.

Lloyd's List (1997). *Polish Register gets ultimatum from IACS.* October 17.

Lloyd's List (1997). *Polska Żegluga seeks bidders.* January.

Lloyd's List (1997). *IACS ponders fate of Polish Register.* October 15.

Lloyd's List (1997). *Major port and yards changes spur maritime sector debate.* May 29.

Lloyd's Ship Manager (1992). *Poland. Special Report.* August.

Lloyd's Ship Manager (1995). *Poland.* August.

Maritime Institute of Gdańsk (1996). *Maritime economy. Short statistic review.* Instytutu Morskiego, Gdańsk.

Misztal K. (ed.) (1997). *Economic reforms. The maritime transport sector in Poland and Germany.* Institute of Maritime Transport and Seaborne Trade, University of Gdańsk and Institute of Transport and Logistics, University of Rostock.

Pawlowski M. (1992). Polish merchant fleet: will it sink or swim? *Rzeczpospolita.* July 7.

Polish Maritime Review (1997). *Pomerania.* June. p 14.

Polish Maritime Review (1997). *The first fast ferry for Polish operator.* June. pp 29-30.

Polish Maritime Review (1997). *Unity Line.* June.

Polish ports handbooks. (1994 - 1997). Link Szczecin, (Annual).

Polska Żegluga Bałtycka (1996). *Polferries - 20 years.* PZB, Kołobrzeg.

Port Development International (1996). *Baltic bridge.* June.

Port Development International (1996). *Fast forward (C. Hartwig).* June..

Poznanski K.Z. (1992). Privatisation of the Polish economy: problems of transition. *Soviet Studies,* 44, 4, 641-664.

Roe M.S. (ed.) (1997). *Developments in the Baltic maritime marketplace.* Ashgate; Aldershot.

Rydzkowski W. and Wojewodzka-Krol K. (1996). *Selected issues in Poland's transport policy in the 1990s.* Paper presented at PTRC Summer Annual Meeting.

Sachs J. (1993). *Poland's jump to the market economy.* The MIT Press; Cambridge, Mass.

Seatrade Review (1996). *Slow progress on Act of Seaports bill.* July.

Seatrade Review (1996). *Well stocked yards but no projects.* July.

Spon N. de (1995). World in focus. Poland. *Fairplay,* May 11.

The Independent (1996). *Chirac wants Poland in EU by 2000.* September 13.

University of Gdańsk (1988). *Maritime transport in Belgium and Poland.* Maritime Transport Economics Institiute, University of Gdańsk and RUCA, State University Center Antwerp, Department of Transport Economics.

University of Gdańsk (1990). *Maritime transport in Belgium and Poland; A state of the art.* Institute of Maritime Transport and Seaborne Trade.

University of Gdańsk (1991). *Shipping and ports in the national economy.* Maritime Transport Economics Institute, University of Gdańsk.

Zurek J. (ed.) (1997). *Maritime transport and its role in the national economy*. Institute of Maritime Transport and Seaborne Trade, University of Gdańsk and Institute of Marine Studies, University of Plymouth.

Appendices

Appendix 1: Focus of the research

Source: Authors

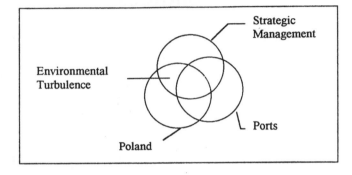

Appendix 2: Models of portfolio analysis

1. The BCG Matrix

The earliest best known model, invented by the Boston Consulting Group, is a growth-share matrix determining market growth rate and relative market share of a SBU by assessing the market's future potential and the SBU's competitive position.

Appendix 2.1: The BCG Matrix
Source: Feurer and Chaharbaghi (1995)

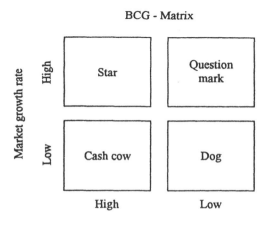

BCG - Matrix

Cash cows, so the suggestion, should be maintained in a dominant position and milked as long as possible. Stars need investment to turn eventually into cash cows. Whereas dogs should be retrenched or divested of, question marks need decision whether to strengthen or divest them (David 1995: 207).

2. The McKinsey/GE Matrix

For GE McKinsey developed a matrix plotting industry attractiveness against SBU strength on a 9-square grid. Since this model gives recognition to a greater number of factors of the environment (Wright et al 1996: 116 or Grant 1995: 411) it is often preferred to the BCG matrix.

Appendix 2.2: The McKinsey/GE Matrix

Source: Feurer and Chaharbaghi (1995)

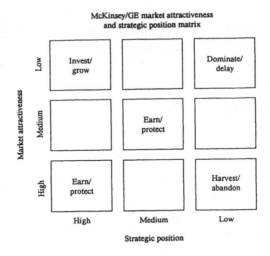

SBU's located in the high ranks should be "built" since they have excellent prospects. Medium profit potential units should be "held". Those which occupy low positions on both axes should be "harvested" (Grant 1995: 412).

Appendix 2.3: The MCC Directional Policy Matrix

Source: Nicholls (1995)

	Low	Medium	High
High	Look for a joint venture	Develop by building the competence	Cherish
Medium	Watch closely, do not delay decision	Maintain but not indefinitely	Allow pursuit by an "intrapreneur"
Low	Discard	Watch closely, do not delay decision	Separate into a subsidiary

Fit with the mission (vertical axis)

Fit with core competences (horizontal axis)

Appendix 3: Proter's five forces
Source: Feurer and Chaharbaghi (1995)

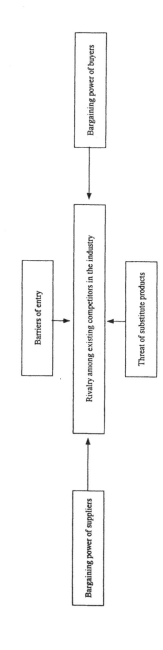

Appendix 4: Generic strategies and strategy clock

Appendix 4.1: Generic strategies
Source: Feurer and Chaharbaghi (1995)

	Lower costs	Differentiation
Broad	1. Cost leadership	2. Differentiation
Narrow	3a. Cost focus	3b. Differentiation focus

Area of competition (Broad / Narrow); columns: Lower costs / Differentiation

Appendix 4.2: Strategy Clock
Source: Johnson and Scholes (1997)

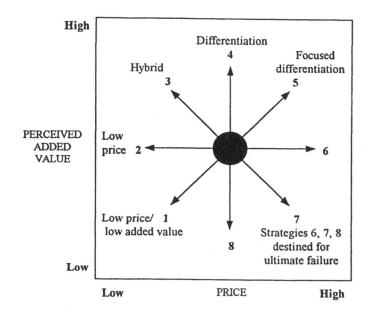

Needs/risks

1	Low price/low added value	Likely to be segment specific
2	Low price	Risk of price war and low margins/need to be cost leader
3	Hybrid	Low cost base and reinvestment in low price and differentiation
4	Differentiation	
	(a) Without price premium	Perceived added value by user, yielding market share benefits
	(b) With price premium	Perceived added value sufficient to bear price premium
5	Focused differentiation	Perceived added value to a particular segment, warranting price premium
6	Increased price/standard value	Higher margins if competitors do not follow / risk of losing market share
7	Increased price/low value	Only feasible in monopoly situation
8	Low value/standard price	Loss of market share

Differentiation

Likely failure

Appendix 5: SWOT

Source: David (1995)

	STRENGTHS - S	WEAKNESSES - W
Always leave blank	1. 2. 3. 4. 5. List strengths 6. 7. 8. 9. 10.	1. 2. 3. 4. 5. List weaknesses 6. 7. 8. 9. 10.
OPPORTUNITIES - O 1. 2. 3. 4. 5. List opportunities 6. 7. 8. 9. 10.	SO STRATEGIES 1. 2. 3. 4. Use strengths to take 5. advantage of 6. opportunities 7. 8. 9. 10.	WO STRENGTHS 1. 2. 3. 4. Overcome weaknesses 5. by taking advantage 6. of opportunities 7. 8. 9. 10.
THREATS - T 1. 2. 3. 4. 5. List threats 6. 7. 8. 9. 10.	ST STRATEGIES 1. 2. 3. 4. 5. Use strengths to 6. avoid threats 7. 8. 9. 10.	WT STRATEGIES 1. 2. 3. 4. 5. Minimise weaknesses 6. and avoid threats 7. 8. 9. 10.

Appendix 6: McKinsey's 7 S
Source: Fifield and Gilligan (1995)

Appendix 7a: Port of Gdynia Holding Joint Stock Company

Source: Kuzma (1996)

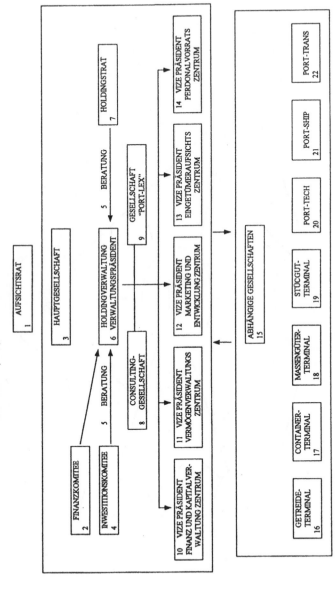

Appendix 7b: Port of Gdynia Key

1. Supervisory Board
2. Finance Committee
3. Holding
4. Investment Committee
5. Advice
6. Managing Board President
7. Managing Board
8. Consulting Company
9. Port-Lex Company
10. Vice President Finance
11. Vice President Asset Division
12. Vice President Marketing and Development
13. Vice President Ownership Division
14. Vice President Human Resources
15. Subsidiaries
16. Baltic Grain Terminal
17. Baltic Container Terminal
18. Baltic General Cargo Terminal
19. Maritime Bulk Terminal
20. Port Technical Company
21. Port Shipping and Supply Company
22. Port Transport Company

Appendix 8: Turnover of Port of Gdynia

Source: Port Gdynia Handbook (1996)

TURNOVER IN PORT OF GDYNIA S.A.

YEAR	1990	1991	1992	1993	1994	1995
Turnover	9967	7263	6279	7759	8005	7633
Polish Foreign Trade Turnover	9157	7026	6097	7066	7072	6727
Transit	810	227	182	693	933	906
Coal	2438	1489	1516	2293	2939	2153
Ore	807	208	153	4	0	77
Other Bulk	1165	1069	739	722	868	857
Grain	1257	784	670	1347	464	527
Timber	1	0	44	16	0	0
General Cargo	3663	3298	2644	3256	3596	3662
Liquid Fuels	636	415	513	121	138	357
Containerised General Cargo	1027	999	901	1051	1141	1326

in 1,000 t

Appendix 9: Turnover in container and ferry terminal 1980-96 and 1991-96

Source: Baltic Container Terminal (1996 and 1997)

1. Turnovers of Terminal in the Years 1980-1995 (without ferries)

year	number of calls	containers in boxes	TEU	total tonnage in ths T	tonnage of containers ths T	tonnage of general cargoes ths T	cars & trucks
1980	105	17.857	23.774	268,2	195,6	b.d.	b.d.
1981	179	27.537	40.033	401,8	329,1	25,9	b.d.
1982	165	30.734	47.477	488,2	414,4	35,1	b.d.
1983	210	39.140	58.637	570,2	498,4	23,8	b.d.
1984	262	47.107	68.150	662,6	591,4	24,3	1.025
1985	360	56.970	79.277	758,6	694,2	18,7	706
1986	347	54.880	76.243	725,7	646,6	29,5	700
1987	473	70.200	96.118	918,8	807,4	45,4	1.490
1988	517	86.259	118.816	1113,8	975,7	75,0	4.992
1989	499	82.642	113.040	1165,4	998,3	93,9	2.179
1990	522	86.375	117.915	1237,4	1018,8	134,0	3.631
1991	535	82.752	114.652	1262,8	991,5	194,6	26.763
1992	802	67.499	97.243	1350,9	895,0	376,6	22.554
1993	828	77.423	114.501	1542,7	1042,6	424,7	21.221
1994	851	80.584	122.139	1732,9	1136,2	503,9	15.282
1995	1000	91.224	140.440	2036,8	1325,7	622,8	30.919
1996	1091	103.341	156.055	2385,9	1552,5	745,0	64.273

2. Turnovers of Ferry Terminal in BCT - Baltic Container Terminal Limited

year	number of calls	number of passengers	number of cars	number of trucks	tonnage of cargo in ths T
1991	133	31.971	6.020	1.579	18.1
1992	316	119.593	21.952	5.000	66.5
1993	189	124.295	19.746	4.527	58.0
1994	217	135.476	17.877	5.947	199,5
1995	352	94.268	14.685	6.556	195,9
1996	306	140.987	22.448	8.582	244,4

Appendix 10: Organisational structure of the Port of Gdańsk
Source: Zarzad Portu Gdansk (1996)

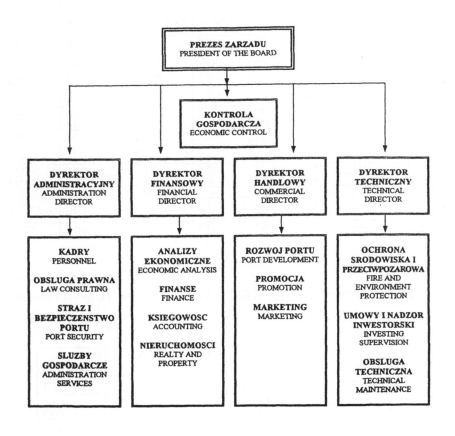

Appendix 11: 1995 Cargo handling by type: Ports of Gdynia and Gdańsk, Port of Gdynia, Port of Gdańsk

Source: Pomeranian Development Agency

1. Structure of cargo handling by cargo type in the complex of the ports Gdansk-Gdynia in 1995 (thousand tonnes)

coal	9273	(35.8 %)
ores	77	(0.3 %)
cereals	664	(2.6 %)
timber	73	(0.3 %)
liquid fuels	6794	(26.2 %)
other bulk cargo	3613	(13.9 %)
general cargo	5408	(20.9 %)
Total	25902	(100 %)

2. Structure of cargo handling by cargo type in the Port of Gdynia - 1995 (thousand tonnes)

coal	2157	(28.2 %)
ores	77	(1.0 %)
cereals	526	(6.9 %)
liquid fuels	357	(4.7 %)
other bulk cargo	855	(11.2 %)
general cargo	3666	(48.0 %)
Total	7638	(100 %)

3. Structure of cargo handling by cargo type in the Port of Gdansk - 1995 (thousand tonnes)

coal	7116	(39 %)
cereals	38	(0.8 %)
timber	73	(0.4 %)
liquid fuels	6437	(35.2 %)
other bulk cargo	2758	(15.1 %)
general cargo	742	(9.5 %)
Total	17164	(100 %)

Appendix 12: Turnover prognosis for Polish ports in 2010

Source: Tubielewicz: Prognosis on Factors determining Development of Gdansk Port-Industry Komplex

Items	1993	2010			2010
		Total	Polish foreign trade	Transit	1993 (%)
Totally	50.5	74.9 - 110.4	66.0 - 83.0	9.1 - 25.1	148 - 219
in that :					
Coal	17.1	16.5 - 22.5	16.0 - 21.5	0.5	96 - 132
Ore	1.8	4.0 - 7.0	3.0 - 6.0	0.1	222 - 389
Other bulk	7.6	9.0 - 12.0	8.0 - 10.0	1.0 - 2.0	118 - 158
in that :					
fertilisers	1.1	4.6 - 5.3	4.0 - 4.5	0.6 - 0.8	418 - 482
sulphur	2.2	1.1 - 2.0	1.1 - 2.0	-	50 - 91
liquid					
chemicals	1.3	2.3 - 3.3	2.0 - 2.5	0.3 - 0.8	177 - 254

Items	1993	2010			2010
		Total	Polish foreign trade	Transit	1993 (%)
Grain	2.5	3.5 - 8.0	3.0 - 4.5	0.5 - 3.5	140 - 320
Timber	0.4	0.4	0.3	0.1	100
General cargo	11.2	17.0 - 21.0	2.0 - 3.0	2.0 - 3.0	152 - 187
in that :					
steel and					
rolling					
products	x	2.8 - 3.4	2.2 - 2.6	0.6 - 0.8	x
containers	1.1	3.2 - 4.4	2.6 - 3.5	0.6 - 0.9	291 - 400
ro-ro	x	6.3 - 8.0	5.6 - 7.0	0.7 - 1.0	x
Crude oil	7.6	20.3 - 35.0	16.0 - 20.0	4.0 - 15.0	263 - 460
Petroleum					
products	2.1	4.0 - 2.5	4.0 - 2.5	-	190 - 120
Gas	-	0.5 - 2.0	0.5 - 2.0	-	-

(in million tonnes)

Appendix 13: Covering letter

Susanne Ferch
Institute of Marine Studies
University of Plymouth
Drake Circus
PLYMOUTH
Devon   PL4 8AA
UNITED KINGDOM

E-mail : sferch@plymouth.ac.uk
Fax : 00 44 1752 232406

Dear Sir

This questionnaire intends to determine whether there is a link between the process of strategy-making (how the port enterprise comes up with its strategies to obtain its competitive advantage in the next millennium) and the perceived turbulence of the business environment (legal, economic, technological, ... conditions), including the transformation process.

This study is a main part of my dissertation on which I am working currently to complete my master course at the University of Plymouth and it is a completely new approach in its field; Professor Michael Roe is my supervisor (e-mail : ims@plymouth.ac.uk). I chose your very port since, as figures show, it is gaining and because Poland has the most dynamic business environment in Europe at the moment.

May I stress that all the information obtained will be treated in strictest confidence.

Taking into account your time, I designed a very condense questionnaire.

Thank you very much for your time and co-operation.

Yours faithfully

Susanne Ferch

Appendix 14: Questionnaire

Questionnaire

Please tick the appropriate answers.

A. Formalia

1. Organisational Structure

Our company is structured in:
        *functional departments   (marketing, finance, operations, ...)
        *divisions   (according to services provided)
        *matrix structure   (according to services and funtions)

At the beginning of/before the transformation process, the company was structured in
        *functional departments
        *divisions
        *matrix structure

2. Hierarchy

The number of levels of hierarchy in our organisation are: 2, 3, >4.

During the transformation process
        *the levels of hierarachy   increased / decreased
        *the number of departments   increased / decreased

3. Number of employees

   (ca.): _____

B. Generation of Strategy

Please consider recently designed strategies e.g. in marketing, development, privatization.

	I strongly agree ... I strongly disagree
1. In general our strategies are developped by ...	
* outside experts	1 2 3 4 5
-called in by us	1 2 3 4 5
-called in by others	1 2 3 4 5
* internal experts	1 2 3 4 5
2. In general we undertake strategy development over time ...	1 2 3 4 5
*incrementally	1 2 3 4 5
*in a flux	1 2 3 4 5
*by transformation	1 2 3 4 5
3. In general our strategies ...	
*are planned and carried out exactly as planned	1 2 3 4 5
*will be adjusted to changes in the environment	1 2 3 4 5
*evolve over time	1 2 3 4 5
*are imposed by ...	1 2 3 4 5
-outside institutions	1 2 3 4 5
-environmental changes	1 2 3 4 5

Appendix 14: Questionnaire, continued

C. The Process of Strategy Development

I strongly agree ... I strongly disagree

1. In general we formulate long-term strategies through

a) a regular planning process, comprising of internal and external appraisal, generation of strategic alternatives, evaluation, choice, implementation and control

       aa) where we use historical strengths and extrapolative forecasts to set operation targets and control operations   1 2 3 4 5

       ab) where we control operations and additionally review the content of our strategies.   1 2 3 4 5

b) constant monitoring of the environment, determining impact and urgency of the changes and deal with them accordingly: high-impact changes are dealt with immediately, medium-impact changes are dealt with in the regular planning cycle; low-impact changes are further monitored.   1 2 3 4 5

c) Sometimes the environment is so turbulent, that previous plans do not apply; a special system to cope with strategic surprises has been created   1 2 3 4 5

d) Process differs from department to department.   1 2 3 4 5

e) The environment is so fast changing that we prefer not to anticipate change but let change happen and react then in real-time.   1 2 3 4 5

f) Combination of the above   please state: _____

2. This has changed over the transformation process   from approach ... to approach ...

D. Hierarchy of Strategic Planning

I strongly agree ... I strongly disagree

1. We employ ...

       a) top-down planning, where management initiates strategy formulation and lower levels implement   1 2 3 4 5

       b) bottom-up planning, where lower levels implement   1 2 3 4 5

       c) interactive approach, where the origin of the strategy formulation is not as important as the interaction between levels.   1 2 3 4 5

2. A the beginning of the transformation process we employed approach ...   a b c

3. The Port Authority determines mission and objectives for the whole port. The operating companies are free to undertake their decisions within this frame.   1 2 3 4 5

4. The Port Authority sometimes advises the operating companies.   1 2 3 4 5

Appendix 14: Questionnaire, continued

5. The directors of the Port Authority and operating companies meet regularly for round table discussions.   1 2 3 4 5

6. Business strategies are developped by all major functional heads jointly, not by a single person / department.   1 2 3 4 5

7. This has changed during the transformation process.   1 2 3 4 5

E. Formality of Planning

	I strongly agree ... I strongly disagree

We have these major plans written down:
*mission	1 2 3 4 5
*objectives	1 2 3 4 5
*budgets	1 2 3 4 5

F. Mission Statement

A mission statement is the most generalised statement about a company capturing its essence of being.

1. What business is your company in? (product, markets, ethos ...)
   Please state:

   _____
   _____
   _____
   _____
   _____
   _____

2. Influences on the content of our mission statement had the ...
*government	yes	no	no opinion
*municipality	yes	no	no opinion
*board of directors	yes	no	no opinion
*port authority	yes	no	no opinion

3. Has your mission statement changed over time?   yes   no
   If so, how?

   _____
   _____
   _____

4. Is having a mission statement of use for a port?   yes   no   no opinion

5. Is there a relationship between having a mission statement and
*improved performance	yes	no	no opinion
*improved marketing	yes	no	no opinion
*improved internal communication	yes	no	no opinion
*better cooperation among management?	yes	no	no opinion

If you do not have a mission statement: Why?
• has to be developped carefully	yes	no	no opinion
• no time, operational management is more important	yes	no	no opinion
• only for times of trouble	yes	no	no opinion

Appendix 14: Questionnaire, continued

- completely useless   yes   no   no opinion

G. Internal Analysis

This section tries to determine what concepts you use to analyse the internal performance of your company.

When we analyse our internal situation we ...   heavily used ... not used

1. look at it in terms of structure, functions and organisational culture   1 2 3 4 5

2. determine internal competitive position via
   - *historical company data   1 2 3 4 5
   - *industry standard   1 2 3 4 5
   - *experience curve model   1 2 3 4 5

3. use competence profiles of these functions
   - *marketing   1 2 3 4 5
   - *finance   1 2 3 4 5
   - *development   1 2 3 4 5
   - *operations   1 2 3 4 5
   - *human resources   1 2 3 4 5

4. use
   - *value chain analysis   1 2 3 4 5
   - *information systems   1 2 3 4 5
   - *7-S framework (strategy, structure, style, staff, skills, systems,shared values)   1 2 3 4 5

5. weigh the strengths and weaknesses of the organisation according to the   impact they have.   1 2 3 4 5

H. Analysis of the External Environment

This section tries to determine how you analyse the external environment of the organisation.

To analyse ...   heavily used ... not used
1. the macro-environment we use ...
   - *PEST-analysis (political/legal, economic, social, technical   2 3 4 5
                        environment)   2 3 4 5
   - *others: _____   2 3 4 5

2. the industry we use ...
   - * Porter's 5 forces model   2 3 4 5
   - *others: _____   2 3 4 5

3. the competitive position we use ...
   - *lifecycle models   2 3 4 5
   - *strategic group analysis   2 3 4 5
   - *market structure positions   2 3 4 5

4. others: _____

Appendix 14: Questionnaire, continued

I. Turbulence of the Environment

This section deals with the environmental turbulence as perceived by respondent.

1. Elements of turbulence

Rating

		high	low
a. Unpredictability
	rapidity of change	1 2 3 4 5
	adequacy , timeliness of information	1 2 3 4 5
b. Complexity | (many factors involved) | 1 2 3 4 5 |
c. Novelty | (circumstances never previously encountered) | 1 2 3 4 5 |

2. Techniques and Tools used to deal with perceived turbulence.   Rating
   What tools do you use to cope with ... ?

a. Unpredictability

heavily used ... not used

data bases, computer models, stastistics   1 2 3 4 5

decision tree   1 2 3 4 5
pay-off matrix   1 2 3 4 5
alternative criteria   1 2 3 4 5

alternative scenarios (degree)   1 2 3 4 5
delphi technique   1 2 3 4 5

b. Complexity

appropriate internal structure: match
structure to:
product range   1 2 3 4 5
customers/market   1 2 3 4 5
combination of the above   1 2 3 4 5
b. Novelty   learn from experience others   1 2 3 4 5
employ outside consultatns   1 2 3 4 5

J. Transformation Process

I strongly agree ... I strongly
disagree

1. We cannot plan strategies effectively for the future since
   privatisation is the all dominating issue.   1 2 3 4 5

2. The Port Authority determines timetable and conditions of final
   privatisation.   1 2 3 4 5

K. Strategic Choice

This section tries to determine how you make your choice between alternative strategies.

I strongly agree ... I strongly disagree

1. When we think of gaining competitive advantage through strategy, we ...
   - think in terms of costleadership, differentiation and focus (specialisation in services / markets)   1 2 3 4 5
   - think in terms of user value / price for customer   1 2 3 4 5
   - thing in terms of growth
     - ◊ high growth   1 2 3 4 5
     - ◊ conservative growth   1 2 3 4 5
     - ◊ neutral   1 2 3 4 5
     - ◊ recovery   1 2 3 4 5

2. Maximizing short-term cashflow is for us at the moment more important than building market share.   1 2 3 4 5

3. We use these tools:
   - SWOT   1 2 3 4 5
   - Critical success factor method   1 2 3 4 5
   - Portfolio matrices (to determine balanced allocation of internal ressources)   1 2 3 4 5   1 2 3 4 5
     - ◊ BCG matrix   1 2 3 4 5
     - ◊ SHELL matrix   1 2 3 4 5
     - ◊ others.   1 2 3 4 5

4. We pursue a direction of ...
   - consolidation   1 2 3 4 5
   - market penetration   1 2 3 4 5
   - market development   1 2 3 4 5
   - product development   1 2 3 4 5
   - diversification   1 2 3 4 5

5. We aim to achieve this with ...
   - development of internal ressources   1 2 3 4 5
   - acquisition of external ressources   1 2 3 4 5
   - joint development   1 2 3 4 5

6. Determination of Decision Criteria
   Do you use these criteria when making a choice between alternative strategies?

   Criterion: heavily used ... not used
   - strategy meets corporate objectives   1 2 3 4 5
   - strategy consistent with policy (culture, ethos)   1 2 3 4 5

   - strategy overcomes weaknesses and threats   1 2 3 4 5
   - consequences of failure   1 2 3 4 5
   - possibility of strategy correction   1 2 3 4 5
   - feasibility of strategy   1 2 3 4 5
     - ◊ financial
     - ◊ marketing
     - ◊ info system
     - ◊ skills

Appendix 14: Questionnaire, continued

◊ staff willingness	
• stakeholders' reaction	1 2 3 4 5
• potential rewards	1 2 3 4 5
◊ market share	
◊ profit, profitability	
◊ financial (ROCE, PBP, etc.)	
◊ enhanced quallity	
◊ improved image	
◊ superior customer service	

7. We use these formal methods when we make our decisions:
   - intuition   1 2 3 4 5
   - qualitative approaches   1 2 3 4 5
   - quantitative approaches   1 2 3 4 5
   - others: _____   1 2 3 4 5

8. The Content of Decision Criteria

   I strongly agree I strongly disagree

   a. The content of criteria has changed over time.   1 2 3 4 5
   b. The criteria are determined by:
      - board of directors   1 2 3 4 5
      - ceo   1 2 3 4 5
      - stakeholders   1 2 3 4 5
      - bank requirements   1 2 3 4 5
      - government   1 2 3 4 5
   c. The actual choice is undertaken by:
      - board of directors   1 2 3 4 5
      - ceo   1 2 3 4 5
      - stakeholders   1 2 3 4 5
      - bank requirements   1 2 3 4 5
      - government   1 2 3 4 5

L. Managing Strategic Change / Implementation

I strongly agree ... I strongly disagree

1. We know our company and employees and can thus easily   1 2 3 4 5
   determine if there is resistance to change and of what kind

2. We prefer to employ formal procedures to manage change via   1 2 3 4 5
   - force field approach   1 2 3 4 5
   - changing systems procedure   1 2 3 4 5
   - changing the control system   1 2 3 4 5
   - changing the reward system   1 2 3 4 5
   - Balanced score card approach   1 2 3 4 5

3. We feel there is/was a need to make the designed process, the   1 2 3 4 5
   reasons and outcome of change public in the company as to gain
   full support of the employees.

4. In order to manage the change successfully, it is sufficient that   1 2 3 4 5
   management alone know about process and outcome of change.

M. Organisational Culture

I strongly agree ... I strongly disagree

1. Management likes to control down to details.   1 2 3 4 5

Appendix 14: Questionnaire, continued

2. This was different at the beginning of the transformation.   1 2 3 4 5

3. Communication in our company is ...
   across departments   1 2 3 4 5
   is across levels   1 2 3 4 5
4. Employees are open for change.   1 2 3 4 5

N. Control

I strongly agree ... I strongly disagree

1. We have a strong feedback system.   1 2 3 4 5
2. We control operational performance.   1 2 3 4 5
3. We review regularly our ...   1 2 3 4 5
   * control system   1 2 3 4 5
   * strategic content   1 2 3 4 5
   * implementation system   1 2 3 4 5

O. Your Evaluation of Strategic Tools and Techniques

I strongly agree ... I strongly disagree

1. Strategy is a luxury. We prefer to denote our energy to technical and operational functions.   1 2 3 4 5
2. Strategy forces into a logical approach to things.   1 2 3 4 5
3. Strategy creates awareness among managers.   1 2 3 4 5
4. How much time does management spend for
   * strategy: _____ %
   * operational tasks: _____ %
5. Has this changed over time and how?
   Time spent for strategic management   increased / decreased.

Thank you very much for your time and cooperation.

Would you like a result analysis?   yes / no

Appendix 15: Annotations relating to the questionnaire

B3	describes the concept of realised, emerging and imposed strategy
C1aa	describes the concept of strategic planning
C1ab	describes the concept of strategic management
C1b	describes the concept of strategic issue management
C1c	describes the concept of strategic surprise systems
C1e	determines whether the organisation uses real-time systems or positioning systems
C1f	The systems are not mutually exclusive; strategic issue management and strategic surprise management can be combined with other strategic systems.
D3-5	try to measure the influence of the Port Authority regarding the development of mission, goal and objectives by the operating companies / subsidiaries
D6-7	measure who in the hierarchy is responsible for strategy making and whether this is done cross-departmentally or single-functionally by one department / person
D8	measures the formality of planning, which is an indicator as to what extent process and content of strategy are conscious in the managers' minds
F1	Answers to this question give insight into how mission of ports adhere to the models developed by literature.
F2	Specific to the situation of Polish ports, these bodies were selected as potentially having influence.
F3-6	measure the subjective evaluation of the use of the mission statement in the port industry
G1, 4, 5	check whether the respondents actually think in those terms as used by literature
K1	analyses which generic strategy concepts are employed in the Polish ports
K4	analyses which directions are pursued by the ports
L9b	relates to D1, F2
c	

For Product Safety Concerns and Information please contact our EU
representative GPSR@taylorandfrancis.com Taylor & Francis Verlag GmbH,
Kaufingerstraße 24, 80331 München, Germany

Printed and bound by CPI Group (UK) Ltd, Croydon, CR0 4YY
08/05/2025
01864408-0002